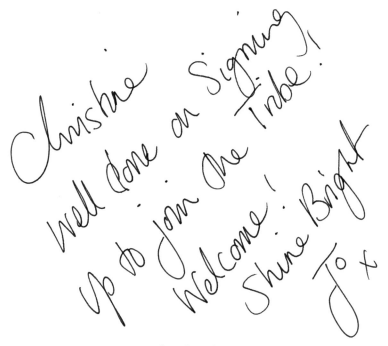

Christine
Well done on Signing
Up to Join the Tribe !
Welcome !
Shine Bright
Jo x

Ask & Act

10 Inspirational tips to get you started on your
Entrepreneurial Journey

By Jo Macfarlane

Contents

Dedication

Introduction

Conclusion

Acknowledgements

Dear friend,

I have always wanted to write a book and share with you the many incredible things that I have been blessed to experience and deepen my enjoyment of life and business.

I am not an expert, a doctor, a coach, a psychologist or someone who is here to tell you what to do and how to be. We are all unique souls, but I wanted to share with you the vast knowledge, techniques and words that I have discovered that have brought comfort, inspiration and belief.

I want to dedicate this book to you. I believe every person has been put on this planet for a reason; to share your hidden talents that you may not have discovered yet and your unique and beautiful gifts with the world for the greater good. I want to reach into that part of you that knows she's a game-changer. I want to appeal to that part of you that is going to put this book down and take action, the part of you that wants to see what she's capable of when she takes action.

I know you want something different, you want some inspiration and a plan. You want to dispel the haters and step outside your comfort zone. You want to go for your dreams once and for all. I'm here to tell you that you already know that somewhere deep within yourself. You just get to ask and act for what you want in life and the rest will fall into place.

Always remember - you might be the juiciest peach in the world but there is always someone who doesn't like peaches.

If you gain one slice on the peach of inspiration from this book, my job is done.

Always shine bright.

Jo x

For Stuart & Archie

What people are saying about Ask & Act

"It's very honest and very real, and that's what makes it different from the run of the mill business books. I really enjoyed it because of that."
Lynda Nicolson

"Your book looks at running a business from a completely different perspective."
I Jack

"It was inspirational just to get on and get stuff done."
J Findlay

"I'm so glad that I had the chance to read your book as I took so much from it to change my mindset at this time."
W Short

"You have written such an inspirational book for not only budding entrepreneurs but for those who have wanted encouragement on

their journey and not been able to find it."
A Carlyle

"I truly loved the journey this book took me on!"
D Novitsky

"I can't wait for your book to be published as I am longing to lose myself in it."
C Niven

"Your tips for success are amazing and ones I will definitely take on board and utilise going forward with my business start up. I loved how the book was so personal and not just another business advice book."
L Clarke

"It is truly inspirational, whether you are starting your own business or just looking for personal inspiration and motivation. I have put in practice a few of the exercises and suggestions and now have a daily mantra and put things out to the Universe."
P Muir

"Loving the book! Feels like we are sitting having a great journey on a train."
E ward

"I have just finished your book and wow, I loved it. There are parts I could have written myself and new ideas and concepts I am seriously considering."
C Watt

Introduction

Hello, it is nice to meet you! I am Jo, and I am delighted you felt compelled to pick up a copy of my book. I can't wait for you to get to know a bit more about me and if you'll allow me to get to know a bit more about you, we can connect over on my social media channels (I'll pop the links at the end of this section).

I am Jo Macfarlane, and I live in Anstruther, Fife, with my husband Stuart and my son Archie. After a few jobs in my teens, I got serious with my career in 1992 when I started my career as a long haul travel flight attendant. I enjoyed 16 years working for Air UK, British Midland and British Airways before embarking on my one true business passion which is my luxury candle business. Working for an airline played to my strength as a people person. I got a real sense of pride and achievement from delivering flawless customer service. I noticed very early on in my career that going the extra mile for people enhanced their overall customer journey and experience, but on a personal level this brought me real happiness, pleasure and job satisfaction.

In addition to my life in the air, I have always been a creative person and one who is very moved by the plight of sustainability and the importance of the environment. I love the old 'make do and mend' mentality, which leaks into many areas of my life. I also love candles and fragrance and found myself staring at empty wax candle votives wondering if I could make candles to put in them, rather than they be destined for tea lights (which don't last long and produce waste from the metal casing). I discovered the wonderful world of wax, wicks and combining fragrance and started hand pouring my own signature scented wax into empty glass jars. This was something of a regular pastime and hobby for me until 2009 when my son was just one, and I decided that this really had potential to be turned into a bright business idea.

I left the security of long haul and took the risk to start Jo Macfarlane Candles from my kitchen table. I have developed my vegan soy luxury candle range to include a variety of sumptuous high-end fragrance and nature-identical oils. I create candles that capture the essence of the countryside and coast with a nod to my native Scotland in every pour. I work with luxury hotels, event managers and weddings in London and across Scotland to create Private Label candles that promise to 'Scent the moment, scent the memory'.

I have taken my love of people, passing on my knowledge and customer service one step further with my candle making workshops. I now have a wonderful studio space where I host small intimate candle making sessions. Attendees of all ages can come and learn to make their own candles in a relaxed, informative and warm, friendly environment. In 2019 I launched my online course to help fellow entrepreneurs turn business ideas into reality through my structured Ignite Your Passion - Build Your Business programme which aims to help would-be entrepreneurs launch their business from their kitchen table in 12 weeks. In 2020, I decided that as part of my dedication to helping entrepreneurs realise their dreams and build businesses that they love, I would write this book and share my entrepreneurial experiences.

My motto is 'If it doesn't challenge you, it doesn't change you'. I adore a challenge, and over the last five years I've pushed my boundaries and my comfort zone to set myself goals in different areas. I am so proud to have completed challenges including reading 100 self-development books in a year, running the equivalent distance of Land's End to John O'Groats, clocking up 1000 running miles in one year, running marathons, duathlons and completed a gruelling 19 hour English Channel swim. 2020 has become my year to focus on yoga every single day and also to write and publish this book for you to read, learn from, take inspiration and utilise my experience and tips in your own beautiful business.

I have thoroughly enjoyed my ongoing journey as an entrepreneur, and I can't wait to share with you everything I have learned. I am proud to be a working mum and to have created a business that is truly in balance with family life and my life as me - not Jo the mum or business owner but Jo, the woman who likes to compete in crazy challenges or maybe save 20,000 local bees. My business does not leave me burned out. It is a true passion that has me ignited every single day to be better and provide an even better experience for my clients. My business has given me the time and motivation to be the very best version of myself - whether I'm wearing my mum, eco-warrior, runner or candle making hat.

Running your own business is one of the most rewarding experiences, yet it comes with many challenges. Being an entrepreneur can sometimes feel like a lonely and isolated experience.

Still, I hope you'll find a friend in me between these pages as I share with you my own life story along with giving you value and things to implement along your own entrepreneurial journey.

Learn with Me

I have several bonuses related to this book which you can download for free at www.jomacfarlane.com.

I run a 12 week Ignite Your Creativity - Build Your Own Candle Business online programme for entrepreneurs like you who need that personal 1:1 guidance and support as you embark on creating your thriving businesses from your kitchen table. To register your interest and apply for the online programme, please visit www.jomacfarlane.com/build-your-business

If you'd like to learn how to make candles, my beginner entry-level Candlemaking Made Easy online course is available immediately via www.jomacfarlane.com/product/candlemaking-made-easy. Once you have completed the beginner course, you can progress onto the Advanced Candlemaking online course.

I believe anything's possible if you have the desire to challenge yourself. I also believe that you can make anything happen and come to fruition with a little bit of magical manifesting and a lot of action. I can't wait to challenge you as I take you through my ten steps for entrepreneurs who are ready to manifest their dream life and business.

Jo x

Follow Me

www.jomacfarlane.com
www.facebook.com/JoMacfarlaneLtd
www.instagram.com/jomacfarlane

Chapter 1

Get Clear

"If you get clear on the what, the how will be taken care of."

- Jim Rohn

What do you want out of your life and why?

It's like the million-dollar question for many, but it is the key to your motivation and the longevity of your business energy. When you have clarity on why you are in business, this will continue to drive your long-term action as an entrepreneur.

A real-world example of the power of your 'why' could be the scenario of wanting to go on a diet. It's a common thing that I'm sure the majority of people will have done at some point in their life. You decide you're going to diet or change your lifestyle. You go to seek out expert help and consult a personal trainer or a diet club, and they say to you "Why do you want to work with me?" or "Why do you want to go on a diet?". The obvious and most common answer is "I want to lose weight."

You might think you want to lose weight. You might think that is the reason 'why' you want to diet, but it isn't. Nobody ever sets out on a diet for the purpose of ONLY wanting to lose weight. There is always a deeper and more meaningful reason, usually emotion-driven, as to the real reason you want to lose weight. The way to find the answer to this is to keep asking the question 'why' until you get to your answer. With this example, common reasons people really want to lose weight is to feel more confident, have more sex appeal, live a longer life for their kids, tackle health scares or look good naked! There are many additional meaningful and more profound reasons.

Taking this principle, let's apply it to your business. You are reading this book right now as somebody who is either looking for inspiration on their entrepreneurial journey or someone toying with the idea of moving into setting up their own business. It doesn't matter what level of entrepreneurship you have attained; it is still vital to know your 'why' at the deepest level possible.

I would love for you to explore this and sit with this a while. Let it smoulder in your mind and then use this as a hypothetical box of matches to ignite your passion in your business whenever you need a reminder of why you're doing it in the first place (and trust me, you will ask yourself this many many many times on your entrepreneurial journey).

You might think you are looking to get into your own business for money, but that is rarely the deepest 'why'. Yes, it is wonderful having a greater earning potential than a traditional 9-5 pm role where the pay is set each month, but while the financial bonuses of owning and operating your own business are potentially limitless, money does not automatically equal happiness.

Some common reasons other people start and maintain their businesses:

- They fall out of alignment with their current employment and know they want to venture out on their own. The 'why' here may be **freedom**.
- They want to have free reign over their creative processes and feel the pride of having something they have created in their hands. The 'why' here may be **to create**.
- They may have an epiphany and wonder "What is all this for?". This can happen when your own mortality is suddenly brought into your consciousness, and you realise you don't want to wait around for the golden clock and the pension. You have a burning desire to bring your business into the world. The 'why' here may be to have a purpose or leave a **legacy**.

For many people, their motivation for starting their business is to follow a dream. A life-changing event often makes people reassess where they are heading with their life. I have worked with people who have been made redundant, suffered a bereavement, had relationship breakdowns or like myself, had children and started a family. Your life as you knew it changes in an instant, and it forces you to rethink your future. You realise that life is not one big dress rehearsal, you are not getting any younger, and it is time to follow that dream you always had.

Your motivation for starting your own business may be driven by your values and what you stand for. There may have been traits in your personality that have been dormant for years that all of a sudden need to be brought into the world. Suppose you do not know your own personal values or that of your business. In that case, I highly recommend you spend a little time delving into these as they will drive many of your business decisions and ongoing motivation. In the accompanying workbook for this book, I have included a short exercise and link to a video on working out what your values are in both your personal life and your business. Once you know what your business stands for and believes in, coupled with your own personal motivation to start and maintain the energy within your business, it makes your business voice one that can be heard and communicated with absolute clarity.

I recently worked on my business and personal values and came up with the following:

Inspire - I love to inspire people with my luxury products and thoughtful scent combinations like salty seaweed and marine notes. I blend my love of Scotland with nature to inspire people through scent. My approach to sustainability is important to inspire this generation and the next into action to protect our planet. I also love to inspire creativity through my workshops and on a personal level with my challenges. People come from all walks of life, sometimes never having made something before, many from the corporate sector; barristers, engineers and accountants. I truly believe everyone has a creative streak in them. They just don't know it yet, and it's about to be ignited. Welcoming three generations to the in-person workshops was undoubtedly a highlight.

Community - I create communities of like-minded people who thrive in my workshops and online programmes. My business operates at the heart of my local community and works hard to uphold the local community values, economy and ecosystem. Visitors from all over the country come to learn candle making and embrace the community spirit while they are here. My online candle making courses are global to engage people to connect across the continents.

Empower - I believe that any person has the power to do what they set their mind to. I empower would-be entrepreneurs to believe in themselves and take the leap into their new business.

Energy - My business energises and never drains me. I love what I do and pass on that energy and enthusiasm to customers, suppliers, followers and the local community.

Knowledge - I believe there is enough for everyone and love to share what I know so that others may experience the joys of their own creative business. I am a lifelong learner, and my curiosity and thirst for knowledge drives me daily.

Knowing your personal and business values will help guide you in the right direction on any future business decision. If you get your values absolutely right, it will make any question you ask yourself easy in the future. Is this supplier right for my business? Do we share the same values? Yes - let's do business. No - we're out of alignment and stand for different things, and this might not be the best business decision. It works when asking if you should invest in anything or any programmes with coaches and mentors. You need to have some common threads of shared values if you're going to work well together.

Getting Clear on What You're Capable Of

Knowing what you can achieve when you set your mind to it holds such power. When you set yourself challenges, and you achieve your goals, you fire up your self-belief. When you fire up your self-belief, you can direct that energy into so many areas of your life - including your business.

If you want to set up your own business, you need to have grit, tenacity, courage and boundless energy. Often, people will start their own businesses as a side hustle while working in full-time employment, or like me, it will begin as a spark of an idea when on maternity leave. You may go through a very normal period of feeling like you're in the juggle struggle and the relentless hustle and grind. My wish for you is that you learn to love this process and realise that the hardships, in the beginning, can be viewed with enthusiasm and passion and they will set you up for your future endeavours.

Too many people give up before realising what they're capable of and that translates across so many different things, whether it's that diet you said you would do, that puzzle you vowed to complete or that business you dreamed you could set up. There will be many points in your business or life that you will hit a plateau. This is the point many people believe they should give up, myself included. I only have to visit my attic to see my unplayed silver saxophone or my skis my friend gave to me on the promise that I would complete my BASI (British Association of Snowsport Instructors) qualification. I might yet become the UK's oldest ski instructor. I have been there, so I know, trust me on this. You need to keep on going beyond the plateau! In the book Three Feet from Gold By Sharon Lechter and Greg Reid, they tell the story of the Darby family who dug for gold. They weren't in the knowledge of the way the gold seams lie. They gave up not knowing that they were literally 3ft from gold because they mined across the seam and not along it. The Darby's sold the land, and the purchaser went on to discover the gold and gain great riches. It isn't just about trying, it is about staying the distance and developing the discipline in the early days that will see you through to your happy and prosperous retirement (hopefully at an early age!). Discipline is being able to force yourself to do something despite how you feel over and over until it becomes a habit.

It takes time to build a habit and discipline. My tips are:

1. Schedule it in with yourself - make it non-negotiable. Set reminders on your phone until it becomes a habit.

2. Don't let another thought get in the way of what you want to do. Don't listen to that negative chatter that goes on in your head saying you're no good.

3. Start with the end in mind, just concentrate on how utterly amazing you will feel once you are done. If it's exercise, roll out your yoga mat, put your swimming costume on, put your trainers on, and you're halfway there!

One of my favourite quotes on discipline is this:

No discipline = no life
Half discipline = half-life
Full discipline = full life

You meet people in life, and sometimes you can see it in their eyes, it is a glimmer of courage or a knowing look that nothing will stop them. They've had steely determination since their childhood; it was probably drilled into them from their parents. They seem to have the unbreakable will.

If you were to look at me now, as I approach my 50th year on this earth, you might look into my soft but resolute eyes as I participate in some of my feats of endurance and think I've always been that way. The truth is, I haven't.

As a child, growing up, my health really held me back. I suffered very severely from asthma (I still do) which resulted in me having to take a lot of time off school during periods where my chronic illness was utterly debilitating.

I was always in and out of school. Looking back, I think being an only child and suffering this terrible condition; my parents placed more emphasis on my recuperation than my education. This was entirely understandable as at times, I struggled for breath, let alone even had the energy to put my school uniform on. On the days when my health was manageable, I would go into school, but teachers possessed the same nonchalance towards my education. "We'll put you in for this exam Jo, but we aren't expecting any great things from you", they'd say with a slightly cocked head, feigning sadness. They had no hopes for me. It was like my health condition had written me off, and nobody had any high expectation for poor little Jo to succeed.

I am a big believer in never blaming anyone else for your circumstances and can look back and realise I wasn't taking responsibility for my own education. If I knew then what I know now, I could've taken matters into my own hands and ploughed myself into my studies. Yet I was young and unaware of the impact this indifference to my studies could have. It came as no shock to anyone, but getting my exam results and realising I'd completely failed some key subjects, including English and Maths was a bit of a blow.

After leaving school, still, in a mode where I was pretty much drifting through life, I decided to retake my Higher English exam by taking night school courses. While studying in the evenings, I noticed there was a wealth of subjects at my disposal if I wanted to try and learn something fresh, exciting and new. My previous experience of learning had not gone too swimmingly, but when I saw that St. Andrews University (yes that's the one where Prince William and Kate Middleton would meet and fall in love) ran night courses in various other subjects, I wondered if I could prove myself and my lack of academic flare wrong. One course caught my eye - Japanese. It looked like a challenge and was completely out of my comfort zone, so I decided to enrol and see how I fared.

My dad had been an engineer in the Merchant Navy and so was often away from home for extended periods of time. On his eagerly awaited return from his lengthy travels, he'd always arrive home, and I'd excitedly watch his black and silver case pop open on the floor. He'd say "See what you can find" and I'd hurriedly rummage through well-worn travel clothes to find dolls, trinkets and unusual artefacts from his global jaunts. Travel always seemed exotic and exciting. Dad would tell me tales of 'buying' items in exchange for his western bar of soap or empty oil drum and paint magnificent pictures of the locals, their cultures and customs in the places he'd travelled. When I wasn't in bare feet on the beach, I was wearing clogs from the Netherlands or Getas from Japan that dad had brought back from his travels. Learning a new language and expanding my horizons from the small Scottish fishing village where I'd grown up was my first step into discipline and determination and the next stage of my life.

I did a year at St. Andrew's University. I completed the following three years of my Japanese course in Reading after landing myself a job as cabin crew for the now-disbanded British Midland airline.

Learning a foreign language ignited something in me that has remained with me for the rest of my life. Firstly, I picked a topic I wanted to study rather than had to study, which immediately felt different. I also realised I would have to self study quite a lot in order to pass the course. This time I was working on my own in terms, keeping myself accountable, I was the only one responsible for my own learning. Yes, I had my classes at the university, but I had to apply myself to complete the work in my own time with no parents or teachers to ensure my work was done. I listened to my language audio tapes in every spare moment I could. I practised my pronunciation and scoured over my Japanese scrawl for hours on end until I felt the new intonation, words, sounds and script was burned into my brain.

I worked hard in the daytime, waitressing in Scotland and then as cabin crew when I lived in Reading. I had to make my studies fit around my job, and when the time came, four years later, to graduate with distinction in Japanese, I was filled with such pride and happiness. After being basically told by my teachers that I had no academic prospects, I'd applied myself, been disciplined and determined and emerged with a qualification in one of the world's most complex languages. I was ecstatic.

Picking up my certificate to say I'd completed and passed my course ignited a curiosity, thirst and obsession for learning that continues to this day. Some may view this as always needing and wanting to know more, never being satisfied with my lot, but I believe knowledge holds the most power for us. It makes us interesting people. It broadens our world and gives us brand new perspectives we may otherwise have no knowledge of.

Around the same time I passed my Japanese qualification, I heard that British Airways were opening up vacancies for UK cabin crew and looking to recruit people who possessed good conversational skills and an overall comprehension of a global language. This was the first time this had happened. Prior to this new and exciting opportunity, cabin crew had been selected for BA on the basis that they had a basic understanding and conversational skills in a European language. I'd spent three months immersing myself in the French language, hoping to be given the opportunity to interview for BA and have enough knowledge of the French language by the time my interview came around. I didn't need to worry, Japanese was now a desirable language for British Airways, so I filled in my application form and visualised getting my dream cabin crew job.

In the same way, I'd applied myself to learning a new language and had started to flex my self-discipline and determination muscles with my self-studies, I had to admit I had no clue about interview skills. On my first application to BA, I failed miserably. For someone who had a great grasp of Japanese as a language, it seemed I had forgotten all of the customs and traditions that are so important as you travel from country to country. I made a terrible mistake - I shook the hand of the Japanese examiner instead of bowing to her as is a custom in Japan. It was an instant fail, and I was devastated. Failing meant I'd have to wait a whole year before applying again. The vision of me in my new dream role faded slightly as I tended to the wounds of my ego at making such a fundamental and costly mistake.

At the time, working for British Midland, we all seemed to want out! Bigger and better airlines were emerging, and enthralling long haul travel to far off destinations became the goal. As I had another year before I could apply to British Airways again, I decided with my trademark determination that I'd use this as a learning experience.

I completed an audit on myself. I reflected on the day with British Airways and my performance in the interview and assessed where I'd fallen short of the requirements, then analysed what I could do to improve the next time I applied.

I decided that I would use the next year to pursue my Japanese skills and improve my comprehension and conversation skills even further. I focused on Japanese at every spare moment. I listened to hours and hours of audiotapes and practised for what seemed like weeks on end.

At the end of that year, I applied to British Airways again. This time I was shocked and saddened to learn I'd passed my language skills and customs with flying colours, but I was deemed not suitable to be offered a job on the 'World's Favourite Airline'.

At this point, I could've chosen to completely give up as I watched many of my peers in British Midland leave after landing their dream jobs. I was confused. I couldn't understand what they had that I didn't.

One day in our British Midland base, I noticed a brown envelope get stuffed into someone's pigeon hole. I watched this same envelope get a little tattier as the weeks went on and it appeared in different people's pigeon holes. A few weeks later, curiosity got the better of me, and I decided to peek inside. There, encased in crumpled up soft cardboard were two books. One of which was 'Great Answers to Tough Interview Questions'. "Bingo!" I thought as it dawned on me that my colleagues who had been successful in leaving British Midland and securing their dream jobs with British Airways had been passing these books around.

I suddenly realised that my previous 12-month focus had all been on the language and where I'd failed the year before. I didn't even stop to think that I might have failed at other parts of the interview process.

Once again I audited myself and played back the last two years and attempts at getting into British Airways. As I started to read the book, I noticed a trend in the tone of the advice.

Positivity.

There was an emphasis on the need to be positive in the interview situation. With advice on how to tackle the tough questions about a difficult boss you'd worked for, or a challenging situation, I almost facepalmed myself as I replayed the image in my mind of me back at my interview. If anyone could write the book on how NOT to interview, I realised it was me. I recalled my previous two attempts at getting into British Airways and saw in my mind's eye what went wrong. I was over-excitable, would flail my arms everywhere, I'd dominate group exercises out of anxiety and wanting to stand out, and the worst - I'd bad-mouthed my company and my bosses in both interviews! That was just the biggest no-no! Someone once said, "You wouldn't run a marathon without training for it, so why would you go to an interview without training for it?"

Reading 'Great Answers to Tough Questions' made me realise I'd not just been interviewing wrong, I'd been living my life wrong too. It was all too easy to get bogged down in the negative. As I practised my interview questions and answers in the mirror, I noticed how I felt in my body and mind as I reframed negative situations into positives. It made me realise all the life lessons I had been through had not been as bad as I thought - not when I decided to see them as positive times in my life where I'd grown professionally and personally.

I devoured 'Great Answers to Tough Questions', and I practised determination and discipline as I prepared for my interview with British Airways. I was well versed in the company, knew what I wanted to say and how I wanted to come across. I was ready for my third time lucky. I applied and received the date for my long-awaited interview.

At the same time, Virgin Atlantic opened up some vacancies on their long haul flights. A friend of mine worked for the airline and even though she knew I was determined to work for British Airways, encouraged me to apply. The idea was if British Airways didn't work out, Virgin could be a Plan B until I was able to interview for BA again. I went to her house. I tried on her stylish red uniform. I practised my interview questions, and she gave me valuable insights into Virgin and what they were looking for.

In the same week, I struck gold and landed an interview for both Virgin and British Airways within days of each other. I felt very lucky to have got through to interview for both, and I was confident that I'd sail through each process. I'd been practising my interview techniques for over a year, having failed in the last two interviews I knew exactly where I'd gone wrong, and I was determined to showcase the true me.

On the day of the Virgin interview, I sat down with the panel, and they asked me the first question. "Why do you want this job?".

"I think I would be perfect for British Airways because..." I stopped. Aghast. With an open mouth, I took a sharp intake of breath at the realisation of what I'd said. I'd been so focused and prepared for getting the BA job I'd completely messed up my Virgin interview. British Airways was imprinted on my brain thanks to all the preparation I'd been doing for months. "Shall I get my coat now?" I asked with a nervous giggle to the panel who were not impressed.

It all worked out for the best, though. A couple of days later was my British Airways interview, and I put every single drop of practice into my time in front of the panel. I sat on my hands to stop them flailing around, and I gently crossed my legs at the ankle, not the knee which is deemed as defensive body language. I talked with positivity and compassion about my role at the time in British Midland. During exercises we'd be asked to discuss what you would take on a desert island with you, not to see what you would actually take but how you interacted with your group. During the practical part of the interview process, we had to build a construction from egg cartons and straws. A voice in my head whispered to me "Create The London Eye". The interviewers frantically started taking notes when I announced confidently what I was going to create. I actually didn't know British Airways had sponsored The London Eye at this point. I think a higher force was looking out for me this day. As the interview process went on, I explained my lessons and growth and sold myself as the right person to join the British Airways team. I was so prepared it was like I was reading from a script in my mind, and I landed the dream job - finally!

Working in long haul travel meant I regularly had down route time. This is when, as long haul cabin crew, you have additional down time at your flight destination. Sometimes that might be 24 or 48 hours in your destination. Sometimes it was an extended break of 7-10 days depending on the flights and the final location. In the aviation industry, due to the demands on the body and mind of long haul flying, suicide and depression are prevalent. A disrupted sleep pattern, different time zones, long hours and then long periods which could often be spent in solitude away from friends and family can have a negative effect on your mental health.

When arriving in places like the West Coast of America or Japan, I'd find that my sleep pattern would be out of whack. I'd often wake at 1 am and then be unable to get back to sleep. Our routine was to meet with other cabin crew around 9 am for breakfast as a team which meant a huge chunk of time alone. This is depression danger time for many cabin crew as the stress of insomnia, jet lag and isolation is not good for brain function.

After finishing my night school courses, I'd continued with my Japanese reading, understanding and conversation audiotapes. I decided to aim for more learning and so started to use my down route time to engage in random courses. I learned how to be a sommelier and even took a course on proofreading!

My routine worked well. I'd wake around 1 am, unable to get back to sleep. I'd take my time showering, putting my makeup on and getting dressed and then just after 2 am I'd start my studies. I'd be able to complete a huge chunk of learning before breakfast with the rest of the team. It meant I didn't have the chance to feel lonely or bored. It gave me a purpose, and I started to marvel at all I was able to achieve when I applied myself.

I enjoyed 12 glorious years flying long haul all over the world. It was a fantastic job that didn't fit a traditional 9-5 pm box. When my husband and I decided to start a family, I had an inkling that long haul wouldn't work in the long run. By the time my son, Archie was a year old, I knew it was something I couldn't go back to. In the same way, I audited myself after those first two devastating interviews with British Airways, I began to audit myself as the new person I was becoming - the mum with a zest for life and thirst for knowledge. What could I do next?

In my current work as a coach, I teach others how to develop a business idea from side hustle to spectacular business. Women join my 12-week programme to learn how to build a business from their kitchen table. One of the first things we do is an auditing self-awareness exercise that I have done so many times throughout my life to better myself. We discuss their skills and all they've acquired in their lives, careers and hobbies. There are life lessons in everything we do, and it is about drawing out those unique skills, qualities and innate talents that make us who we are. Then it is time to transfer them into something new and a new business direction.

I realised after leaving my life in the skies that I had a batch of skills and knowledge that could be transferred to many different industries and businesses. I had ingrained impeccable customer service skills running through my veins, I believed in a highly personalised approach, I was patient and calm, and I had a thirst for knowledge and determination that had been formed during my 'down route' time (my time off flying) where I had dedicated my free time to continued self-study.

My candle making business has always thrived on these very skills that I have acquired over my working lifetime. I believe in a bespoke and personal approach - no two customers are ever the same. I believe in quality, so I use the finest sustainable and environmentally sensitive ingredients which blends my love of luxury with my personal mission to be as environmentally conscious as possible. I have the patience, understanding and calm manner to now be able to teach candle making to others. I believe in sharing your wins and watching others flourish, so I deliver an online course in the art of setting up and running your own business through my Ignite Your Creativity 12-week course.

On writing this book, it has allowed me to reflect on my life and realise that all roads have led to this point. I needed to achieve things, turn my back on the negativity displayed to me by my teachers and discover the joy of learning for myself. I have come to realise that challenging yourself and getting out of your comfort zone is one of the most rewarding feelings in the world. It is this phenomenal feeling that has seen me get out of my comfort zone in life, business and with my fitness. I am just an ordinary mum and wife from a small village in Scotland, and I'm here to say that if I can do it - you can too.

You might be reading this and be able to reflect on a time when you got yourself out of your comfort zone. Maybe you set a weight loss goal, or you renovated your house, or you set up your own business. Perhaps you set lofty fitness goals like me. The excitement of setting goals, then consistently following through with your actions, is utterly enthralling. You emerge with a sense of pride and achievement that becomes addictive. That is why I always have some kind of challenge on the go in my own life - to make sure I don't rest on my laurels and continue to push my boundaries. I talk about this in more detail in Chapter 9 - The Work-Life Challenge.

I am writing this book as another way to get out of my comfort zone and also try and help you, my reader, get clear on what you want, why you want it and how you can achieve it. I'm clear in what I want to say to you in my head, but it feels much more terrifying putting words on paper like I am laying myself bare, but I hope it helps you see that we are all capable of so much more than we realise.

- Taking action into the unknown takes a significant amount of bravery and determination.

- Taking action consistently, until it becomes a flawless habit, takes self-discipline.

- Taking action and taking that first small action step has the potential to change your life.

- It just starts with one small action.

- Once you know what it is you want and why taking that first small action becomes deeply exciting.

Are you ready to take action into your entrepreneurial journey with me?

Exercise - Taking Action and the Smallest Action Step

- What would you love to do in your business? What would you love to do or learn or get started?

- What has stopped you from taking that action step so far?

- What is the one thing you could do right now to take action on achieving your most important and pressing #1 business goal?

Chapter 2

Expand Your Horizons

'You cannot discover new oceans until you have the courage to lose sight of the shore'.

When you set out in business, when you make that leap into entrepreneurship, you immediately embark on a journey of new places, faces, processes, challenges, lessons and joy. When you own your own business, no two days are usually the same and no matter how long you have been in business, every day is an opportunity to learn and grow.

Having an open mindset is vital in any business owner. Having a closed or fixed mindset will close doors in your face before you've even attempted to try the door handle. Having an open mind is important along with dropping the ego, the assumptions and the limiting beliefs that will stand in your way of both personal growth and the growth of your business.

I am a firm believer in expanding your horizons. Having arrived in entrepreneur-land from a travel background, leaving to go on adventures in both the logical and metaphorical sense in life and business is where you find new paths.

I encourage you to expand your horizons, and this chapter is broken down into three thought-provoking parts: in the following ways:

1. Expanding your horizons in your home country and foreign travel to experience new cultures
2. Through your continued education and learning to glean valuable knowledge
3. Through your connections to like-minded people who can support you

Curiosity is the thread that weaves through each of these points. I know that staying curious means you're always growing and learning. Having a thirst for knowledge or a desire to experience different cultures and ways of being will ensure you continue to live a rich and full life. You cannot get bored when you continue to learn. There is nothing more exciting than embarking on an adventure, whether that be through learning something new, connecting with someone who you align with or heading out to visit and experience a new or unusual international destination.

Part 1 - Expand Your Horizons - My lifelong love affair with travel

'Blessed are the curious for they shall have adventures.'
- Lovelle Drachman

Do you love to travel? To seek out adventures and find new places?

To expand your horizons and get out of your comfort zone?

I feel very strongly that once you have travelled, the voyage never ends. I have wanderlust, which is described as 'the strong desire to wander, travel and explore the world'. When you travel, your curiosity is stirred, and your thirst to experience more amazing places continues. I love the ancient Taoist saying 'The journey is the reward'. That is the same in business. You don't start in business thinking you are getting to a destination. It is the journey of your business day to day, week to week, month to month and year to year that is ever-changing and exciting.

Before embarking on my business venture, I enjoyed 16 long years working as cabin crew for British Midland and British Airways. My extensive experience of travel has shaped me into the person I am today, and I feel that travel is the only thing you can buy that truly makes you richer. I am so grateful for all my travel experiences. I got the chance to see the world and experience so many places and cultures in one short span of time. I know that travel has changed me as a person to my core. I don't know if I would constantly seek new adventures in life and business right now had I not caught the travel bug through my career in the aviation industry.

To me, travel has always been something exhilarating. My first memory of travelling on a plane came when I was eight years old. I had won a competition to appear on the TV show Magpie for a whole series, and the TV production company would pay for my mum and me to travel by train to and from London for the broadcasts. This one particular time in London ahead of the broadcast, I got myself worked up. I was about to be sworn into my Brownie Guide pack. At just eight years of age, this was a huge deal to me. I had my Brownie

Guide promise and law memorised in full, and I was so excited about becoming a Brownie and joining my pack. Yet being in London for the transmission of Magpie would mean I would be late back and miss my inauguration ceremony. I was beside myself. There were tears, and my bottom lip stuck out so much it was hard to ignore. The production company kept on asking my mum if I was OK and she waved them away to say I was fine. The wailing got a bit too much, though, and mum revealed to the Magpie team that I was upset at missing being sworn in as a Brownie. They were so kind and accommodating and arranged for us to fly home from Heathrow to Edinburgh instead of the long train home. Mum was so embarrassed, but I was so excited. Not only would I be heading home to become a Brownie, but I was travelling on an aeroplane! I remember it feeling so invigorating, noting the power of the plane and the noises and the feel of the thrust of the engine. We were home so quickly, and I made it to my Brownie meeting on time.

As a child, we didn't travel much outside of Scotland. My dad had enjoyed his career in the Merchant Navy and so when he was home our holiday time was spent in the North of Scotland. Even though the Northern parts of my home country are some of the most beautiful places I have had the pleasure of experiencing, I think living in a tiny country in colder climates pushed me to expand my horizons and embrace my career with long haul travel.

When I would fly to different destinations, we often enjoyed a period of down route time (free time). When I wasn't learning a language or immersed in a course, I used the time to immerse myself in the local communities and experience the culture of different nations first hand.

The great thing about having down route time in far off destinations is that we were still being paid. We might have ten days before we had to fly again, but for those ten days we were still being paid, and we would get an allowance for each day we were in our destination. The allowance payments varied wildly from £7 a day for Harare in South Africa to up to £120 a day for Narita in Japan. As I was so junior in my role as cabin crew, I didn't always get the best routes which meant by default I ended up spending a lot of time in Africa. I didn't mind this at all. I was naturally nosey and loved to explore and found that those who headed to Africa would end up partying and socialising more. We'd fly down overnight and then have the day to relax and the evening to party. While those in Japan, due to the flight time and then the time change, wouldn't socialise as much.

When you were on the flights, your fellow cabin crew would be organising activities on their down route time. Someone might suggest white water rafting or exploring a local destination by boat. You could pay £1 a month to be part of the British Airways BA Equipment club. It meant that when you landed at your destination, there would be a folder of activities or equipment you could borrow. It belonged to British Airways, and as you were a paid-up member of the equipment club, you could access things like bikes, boats and excursions.

Many of the crew who had been flying for years simply liked to relax on their down route time. They'd sit by the pool socialising or get their nails done. I found it a struggle to do this when there was so much to see and do. I loved hearing the stories my father would tell me on his return from his merchant navy trips, and I think this shaped my own quest for experiences. I felt it a waste to visit a place and never leave the confines of the hotel compound or the resort.

I also knew that at any point, my routes might change and I might not get the chance again to visit somewhere or experience a new destination or activity. I had been putting off visiting the Taj Mahal, and on the one trip I decided I would visit the Wonder of the World, the trip had been discontinued. I became very open to all new suggestions of trips and destinations that would be on someone's dream bucket list. I had many of these places at my disposal, and I was going to start to say yes to more opportunities. So when my fellow cabin crew member and friend Helen suggested a camping safari trip in Africa at the Chiawa Camp, even though I detested camping, I jumped at the chance.

We hired a speed boat to take us up the Zambezi river to the camp located in the heart of the Lower Zambezi National Park. It was luxuriously set up with thatched and tented accommodation adjacent to the river where vervet monkeys and an endless parade of birds enjoyed life on the river bank. On disembarking from the boat, we were greeted by elephants roaming through the camp or seeking shade under the nearby forest of mahogany and acacia trees. Views of the Zambezi River Valley took your breath away and also instilled a little fear as the alligators and hippopotamus would eye us up from the river banks and look menacing. Helen headed on a canoe trip at one point and cut it short, terrified of being eaten by a hippo (for they are the most feared creature in the waterways). Open-air showers were always also inhabited by ugly white frogs who would stare at you with their big gloopy eyes and put you off your daily wash! The actual safari side of things was an unforgettable experience. We headed out in converted jeeps to watch the majestic animals at sunset and sunrise. The jeeps would convert at the back into a pull-down bar, and we'd enjoy sundowner cocktails and a cheeky gin overlooking the natural habitat of some of the world's most endangered but intriguing creatures.

Armed guards patrolled the camp and one night I woke with a start. I could feel the warmth and hear the heavy breathing of a giant creature nearby. It stopped, and only a slither of canvas tent separated us. I froze in complete fear and whispered "Helen, did you hear that?" As my hands gripped the covers. "Shush" she hissed back at me without a hint of sympathy for my fear and obviously absolutely terrified herself. I could see the outline of a vast, powerful body and could smell the faint dog-like smell of the huge creature close by. A slight rasp emerged from its throat as it huffed, puffed and moved on its way. We heard the guards stir and the beast was gone. I didn't sleep a wink that night and emerged at dawn from my tent with trepidation. "It was a lion" we were informed by the camp staff as they showed us the giant paw prints across the camp and directly next to our tent. I realised just how close I'd been to one of the world's most dangerous animals!

This experience most definitely shaped my travel excursion choices to this day. My son and husband love to go camping, but my terrifying brush with a real-life Mufasa in a tent in Africa has seen my camping days well and truly archived. I did promise my son that I'd get out of my comfort zone and spend one night in the tent in the garden. I attempted it this year to find myself still awake at 3 am so quietly crept into my cosy bed in the house. After all, there are no lions in Scotland. Or so I hope!

In my career in the long haul flight business, I worked out that I had visited over 190 cities and sometimes more than once. Of all the places I have visited, New York City has to be my all-time favourite place.

I love New York because of the vibrancy. It is a city that doesn't care who you are or where you've come from - regardless of your age, background, race and intelligence, you will always feel like you fit into New York. I remember being in New York in the early 2000s and an article saying there were over 40 different nationalities within Manhattan. When a place is so diverse and multicultural, you feel at home in that energy and welcoming space.

I loved exploring New York in different seasons. It always felt different every time, as the city had something else to give. I adored expanding my thinking and comprehension in culture spots like the Guggenheim Museum. From the moment you see this building from the outside, you are intrigued. This architectural masterpiece designed by Frank Lloyd Wright is now part of the UNESCO World Heritage List but inside is where you expand your thinking. The moment you step inside this building (which looks like a stripey soup bowl from the outside!) you're encouraged to remove all judgement and surrender your thinking to the various pieces of modern and contemporary art.

If the intelligence of trying to decipher modern art becomes too much, there are places where you can't help but feel good and get immersed in the energy and buzz of the city. One of my favourite spots is the Ellen Stardust Diner where up and coming actors and actresses, with a dream to star on Broadway, lend their talents to waiting on and entertaining while they serve you. Set on the corner of 51stSstreet and Broadway in the iconic Times Square, you can't book at Ellen's so expect to queue up around the block to get in. It is well worth it! Take your seat under the bright lights and glitter disco ball, enjoy some of the world's best diner food including the world-renowned milkshakes and desserts while the waitstaff will sing to you, do the splits between the tables and dump confetti on you.

I was lucky enough to travel to New York very regularly - so much so that you occasionally met the same passengers. I adored my time flying in all cabins but maybe mostly First Class because you got to spend a little bit more time with the customers. At the time I was travelling long haul with British Airways, there were 12 flights a day to and from New York. Having so many flights meant having so many staff. So many staff meant needing accommodation for those workers. To solve this problem, BA built their own hotel in New York specifically for cabin crew and BA staff. Called The Concord Hotel it was a real conveyor belt of BA staff and therefore a safe and secure spot for us to base ourselves in the city.

I flew as long haul cabin crew but despite the distance travelled, sadly, I never got to fly to and from New York on Concorde, and this is one of my big regrets. Even though New York was a long haul destination with an average flight time of 5 to 6 hours, the speed of Concorde could get passengers from London to New York in 2 hours 52 minutes and 59 seconds, so unfortunately for me, the Concorde flights were classed as short-haul. I got to sit on Concorde once when it was parked next door to one of our aircraft and was struck at how much it felt like a toilet tube! The minute tiny features of the plane and the passport size windows felt very claustrophobic. Due to the condensed size, it meant the crew would have to pretty much serve everyone by hand from the back - no trolleys! I didn't get to work the route nor experience it as a passenger before Concorde was retired in 2003, but I was lucky enough to watch its last commercial flight into Heathrow, and I'm not ashamed to admit it was very emotional.

I always wanted to take every opportunity I could to explore every destination I visited. As a blonde-haired blue-eyed woman, I have often attracted attention in many destinations where I have travelled—particularly India, Tel Aviv, Japan and even Portugal. As a child, I was on my dad's shoulders in Portugal, and people wanted to touch my light blond hair as they couldn't believe it was so white! I think that's why I enjoyed New York so much because it feels so multicultural that I can blend into the background. Yet one place where blending into the background felt completely alien and uncomfortable was the Middle East. It was custom for us, western women, to cover up in some of these countries. BA issued us with our own Abaya garment, which is a black cloak which loosely covers the whole body except for the face. I was so awkward wearing this. I would really struggle to walk in it and carry items while wearing it. I was so ungraceful, and it was always hot, so it was very uncomfortable. Blending into the background in this way didn't feel as comforting as it did in New York. It felt oppressive, although I have since learned that these cultures and customs are often viewed as a heroic way to protect women, not oppress them. For example, the custom of men walking a step ahead of women does not originate from a need to show that men are superior to women, but the men would walk ahead of their wives in case they encountered danger like a snake in the road.

I sometimes feel there are parallels from my travel days to modern life as a woman running my own business. I often have to make the leap and get out of my comfort zone and take unknown steps in order to get to the places I want to go to. That same trepidation and slight excitement are the same whether you're getting a local bus in the middle of a fishing village in Spain or you're launching a new product. You are hoping that you've taken the right step, but you won't know until you embark on the journey.

In my work selling luxury candles, workshops and courses, I have to know and read my audience. In the same way, when you travel, you have to observe the local people to adjust to the right cultures and customs. I need to learn what is the 'norm' or 'expected' for my customers, in the same way, I learn that the Japanese don't like to be tipped or Indians sometimes shake their heads when they actually mean "Yes". It is about getting yourself familiar with those around you and then fitting the mould. You learn by travelling and experiencing new places that a closed mindset doesn't work. You have to be open to new ways of doing things. For example, for the modern-day shopper, the environment and climate change have become a hot topic; people care about recycling and sustainability. It is important to them. So when I decided to go as green as possible in my business, I did this because I believe in it, but the positive side effect is that my customers appreciated my move towards this.

In my business, I can't hide away. Yes, it might be safer to blend into the background, but that isn't going to get me noticed and help me market my products and services. Covering myself like I had to in some Middle Eastern countries didn't feel comfortable, but in business, I will sometimes metaphorically put a dark cape over myself and my message in my marketing. Is it good enough? Am I getting across what I'm trying to say? What are my competitors doing? It is really easy to think you're doing it all wrong and so do nothing to market your business. You ended up overthinking it so much, wanting it to be perfect, that you do nothing at all - especially on social media. Sometimes it is easier to hide away than let yourself be visible. It is easy to hide away for fear of judgement than step into the light and do what you were born to do.

I also found that travelling opened up a whole world of poverty and pain that I had no idea existed. This has taught me the most valuable lesson of making a commitment to do my part and make small changes to help impact the world. Viewing poverty first hand made me realise we all have a place in the world and that while you might want to force your Western version of change or throw money at the poverty you see, you can't change too much too quickly as negative repercussions could happen for people. My time in India often left me feeling heartbroken and helpless at the poverty on the streets - especially the children. My long haul travel days would sometimes allow for me to take my mum to far off places. One day in India she saw a maimed child begging in the streets and wanted to give him $10. While I knew this would be a life-changing amount of money for him, I knew it could also put him in a dangerous situation. So while $10 was nothing to my mum, I gently encouraged her to give a couple of rupees and look into ways we could use our time and energy to make a more significant overall difference.

Mum and I also took a trip to the source of the Nile. At the source, there was the Bujagali Falls which was a terrifying body of water. You would be dubious about white water rafting there, never mind what I am about to tell you. We got to the Falls and were approached by a group of young children. They said "We swim the rapids for you" and we innocently replied "Oh really?" and then that was it. We were bombarded, parted with $5 and let them show us what they meant. Before we could protest, they had tied a large jerry can to themselves by a rope and jumped off the falls into the whirring, angry water. It felt like time stood still as we held our breath for the small boy, who must've only been about seven years of age, to emerge from the water. This was during a time in my life when I didn't have children myself and looking back; I can't believe we let ourselves get involved in this. It was genuinely death-defying. The jerry can he had tied around his little waist was filled with air. Thankfully after what felt like the longest few minutes, it popped up like a jack-in-the-box out of the water, and the small hands emerged grasping onto it for dear life. He beamed his bright white smile in what felt like a "Ta-dah!" showman moment, and I let myself breathe deep in sheer relief. We both felt guilty about paying to participate in something so foolish and dangerous.

Our driver told us about a person he knew growing their own coffee beans. My mum's wonderful friend Etta was a primary school teacher, and mum thought taking coffee beans back to her would be an excellent lesson for the pupils to see how the beans were grown. My mum was about to offer a lot of money for a sprig of the coffee bean plant, but it was our driver who stopped her, saying that he had bars of soap to swap in exchange for the plant. She did give some money, and the woman was ecstatic, she explained to our driver that she was going to head back to the market to buy a feast with the next day being Christmas Day. I am always mindful that you can't expect to go to a country, intrude on the local culture and expect to change everything. There's a certain rudeness about placing your own western judgement on the customs and cultures of countries where these traditions have been passed down through generations.

This theme overarched my whole career in travel. I often felt devastated that you can't change the world. British Airways often supported orphanages and organisations close to the hotels that we stayed at. I always tried to visit when I flew into these destinations as it was a chance to demonstrate my kindness and do a little good. I would fill my suitcases with knitted booties, hats and jackets which the local ladies from my village in the UK knitted and take them to the orphanages. I had to accept that even though my gesture was small, a small gesture of kindness is all that often matters. I couldn't adopt every orphaned child, even though it pained me in my heart to see them there without their own mothers and fathers. I remember once meeting a boy in Dubai who had been a jockey for camel racing. He was a tiny thing, obviously malnourished and couldn't have been more than 12 years of age. He wasn't entirely sure if his parents had sold him to the camel owners or if he had been abducted, but he accepted that this was his life and had to make the most of it. I recall being in tears along with the rest of my party hearing this boy.

Pat Kerr MBE is a former British Airways air stewardess who, like me, would stay in 5-star luxury in third world countries during down flight time. In the early '80s, Pat became acutely aware of the miserable conditions surrounding many of the luxury complexes in which she rested between flights. She took five months unpaid leave and set up an orphanage in Dhaka in Bangladesh. She got other BA crew members involved in their own down time, and even British Airways supported her to build a new orphanage. It was threatened with closure, so she quit her jet-set lifestyle and moved out to Bangladesh permanently. With the support of the then Chair of British Airways, Lord King, Pat went on to build Sreepur Village - a permanent home for impoverished mothers and the orphaned children of Dhaka. The cabin crew formed the BA Staff Dacca Orphanage Project, which I have been proud to support for many years.

I visited this place a lot and was always so proud to see the children thriving and having a better life. One thing always struck me too, even though the orphanage was a charity, the 500 children in attendance were taught about the importance of charity inside and outside the orphanage. Even though they were in a charitable position themselves and needed support, the children would save a few eggs each day and donate them to another local worthy cause. When you see orphans giving away a bit of their 'wealth' and goods to others, it instils a real sense of charity in your heart, and I've been proud always to prioritise charitable giving thanks to this wonderful experience.

Travel is about finding new places, new people, new food, new sights, new smells and new experiences. It creates the most wonderful memories, the most engaging stories, but it also changes your personality, broadens your understanding of the world and makes you more compassionate. Travel is about constant change and embracing it. I love to be stimulated by travel and would travel my whole life if I could.

Even though I've travelled the world over, I have three specific goals when it comes to travel. I'd like to stay on Richard Branson's Necker Island, travel on the Trans Siberian Railway from Moscow to the Far East almost 6000 miles, and I'd like to sail around the world from Southampton to Southampton. More about those in my chapter on visualisation and manifesting your dreams.

My Top Travel Tips

As a lady with hundreds of stamps from over 50 different countries across many passports, allow me to share with you my top tips for travel;

1) Do it!

Somebody I know doesn't even have a passport. This makes me so sad that they've never experienced new places and cultures. They're missing out on so much more global knowledge and the chance to fill themselves up on everything that is out there. I know some people are terrified of flying, but there are other ways of visiting new places that you could consider like by train or boat.

2) Reconsider the All-Inclusive Holiday

While an all-inclusive holiday offers terrific value and often 5-star luxury with the most convenience and cost savings, the real value is beyond the resort gates. Staying in one place for more than a few days and not seeing the sites can get very dull very quickly. Not meaning to be judgemental but it makes me so sad when people excitedly mention that they have been to Mexico and they have literally flown into the country, bussed to the resort and sat by a pool for two weeks.

If you can, live like a local. Yes, your coffee might be free at your all-you-can-eat breakfast buffet, but there's nothing like finding a local cafe, giving back to the local economy and watching the locals go by. You can't beat the buzz and energy of somewhere like that. I'd look to sit beside a local too. I know that Costa Coffee have put cards on tables that say "I'm open to conversation, come and sit here" which is good to open up connections and conversations.

When I am away, I enjoy getting the local newspaper and even if I can't understand everything I can use my phone to translate or look at the images and get a sense of what is happening. It is much better to place yourself at the heart of the action and feel like a part of it, rather than sheltered away like an outsider.

Chatting to the locals, using local transport and visiting places off the usual tourist track can bring about some brilliant exchanges with people. Just always be on your guard while letting your guard down (I know that sounds contradictory, but I hope you understand what I mean). One time we were a bit silly in Caracas in Venezuela, and we got taxis to a glassware market. We didn't take note of the hotel we were staying in, so we didn't know how to get home. We just had to get the taxi driver to drive back to the centre of town and drive us around until we noticed something familiar and found our hotel!

3) Keep Your Guard Up

Yes, let your guard down enough to explore but keep it up enough to protect yourself. In any city or populated tourist, destination scams happen. From pickpockets to overpriced goods there's always something to catch out unsuspecting tourists. There's also the rule of "If it's too good to be true it probably is!" that is worth remembering.

One time in Hong Kong, my fellow cabin crew colleagues and I had planned to head to a market to buy designer goods and leather bags. When we got there, the market had been shut down. Visibly disappointed, a local man noticed our surprise at the lack of market and ushered us to a building where he promised us the goods and bags we were seeking. We should've known something was up when he took us to the 13th floor of this building by elevator but then walk down the fire escape to his floor below. This was the point where the guard should've come up, and our internal warning sirens kicked in!

He led us into a tiny flat that was packed floor to ceiling with fake luxury goods, and his wife sat on the floor, preparing food. We knew it wasn't for us, but he was persistent and very forceful. All of a sudden there we were, a group of tourists alone in a small flat feeling threatened. We quickly made our excuses that we needed to get money and would be back, but he insisted on coming to the cash machine with us. We practically ran down the 12 flights of the fire escape to get us back out onto the street into what felt like safety.

Also on the topic of the fire escape, I ALWAYS walk the fire escape route in any hotel I'm staying. When I arrive at my hotel, I check the image on the door and then walk the route out counting the doors to the exit. It takes a matter of minutes, but it can save your life in an emergency. I leave the room key by the entrance to grab on exiting so you can always come back to the room. I leave the bathroom light on permanently too so that I can orientate myself quickly on waking. When travelling to up to three different destinations in a week, you could easily forget where you were on waking, which could be quite disturbing. I once woke at 6 o'clock and had to ring down to reception to ask if it was AM or PM. It would also keep the cockroaches at bay and wasn't a shock to see them scatter when you put the bathroom light on.

You should always make a note of routes if you head out and if you have forgotten or haven't booked your own accommodation, make a note of your hotel name and room. On my first visit to Vancouver, Canada, I left the hotel after breakfast to wander the city and realised after a couple of hours; I didn't know the name of the hotel. The room key card can sometimes reveal, but it didn't - awkward! Should I call British Airways in London to ask them? The hotel had a sea view; I remembered that. So after a bit of wandering along the waterfront, I was relieved to be back at the hotel. On another trip to Phoenix, Arizona, we hired a large people carrier, and I drove as I was the only person to bring my drivers license with me. We headed to a local National Park but what we didn't do was get the return directions - cue darkness and driving while jet-lagged in an automatic car on the unfamiliar right-hand side of the road! It was a disaster. We called the hotel, and they guided us back. I always find when I am tired, or in a quick-thinking situation, I have to stay so super calm and focused.

4) Pack these three weird things

I always pack three of the weirdest things you could imagine; a hot water bottle, a coat hanger and a bath plug.

Why? I hear you ask! Well, the hot water bottle is for comfort; especially when you're not feeling great. Even though you may be in a sweltering country, sometimes the air conditioning can make your room feel a little chilly, so the hot water bottle always helps take the edge off a cold room. I always pack one myself in my case because have you ever tried asking the hotel staff in a Caribbean country for a hot water bottle? They look at you like you're insane when you explain what one is. When I used to travel long haul I'd fill up empty water bottles with warm water and use those as my hot water bottle equivalents; you could use this as a barometer of how long you had been sleeping in crew rest, if the bottle was cold you'd slept and most probably time to get up.

The coat hanger is for steaming your clothes. When you arrive at your hotel, most places have fixed hangers in the wardrobe. Having your own coat hanger would allow you to put your outfit in the bathroom, turn the shower on hot and steam the creases out of your clothes.

Although we had our uniform dry cleaned complimentary at every destination, it was great for our off duty clothes.

A bath plug is always essential. I take a rubber bath plug that fits into every bath. It's a rubber disc that lies flat over the plughole, once you run the water the pressure of the water sinks the rubber bung into the plughole, and you can enjoy a bath. Many hotels have removed the plugs to avoid potential flooding of bathrooms, but if you're someone who loves a bath, you better pack your own bath plug!

5) When travelling, travel in dark clothes.

Personally, I always travel in black, especially when going long haul. I like to dress reasonably smart and usually pop a tailored jacket over a black polo or a black t-shirt. I always feel incredibly dirty after travelling, and the black stops any stains showing through. When you've been eating off a tiny aircraft table, or you've experienced turbulence or the sudden jolt of the person in front of you, it is too easy for spillages and stains to happen. So don't wear white (I know a lot of people like to so they can show off their tan) but it's quite embarrassing spilling red wine all over yourself and then having nothing to cover it when you land.

I also wear slip-on shoes as they are easy to take on and off at security and on the aircraft, I pop some cosy cashmere socks on as my feet always get cold. I always try to wear a couple of layers - even if I am flying somewhere hot. I like to bring a pashmina too as it doubles up as a blanket if you end up in a draughty area or you can put it over your head if you want to sleep.

I also carry earplugs, an eye mask, lip balm, toothbrush, sleep spray or Tisserand wrist roller ball, extra water, books, earphones and snacks. Always be prepared!

6) Be kind to everyone!

This is so important. It costs nothing to be kind and even though on the whole people were lovely in my career with BA, at times people would treat you appallingly. If you ever want to get an upgrade then being nice helps. Occasionally on some of my flights in the past, the service director would mention that they are over catered in First Class or Business Class and is there anyone we would like to upgrade from our cabin. You would always pick the person who had been chatty and lovely. I talk about this in more detail and how kindness can change your brain structure and be good for your immune system in Chapter 8 - Be Kind.

7) Pack like a pro

When packing your clothes for travelling, don't fold them - roll them. This will ensure fewer creases in your clothing, and it also gives you extra room in your suitcase. When travelling and staying in hotels, collect the thin plastic shower caps that nobody uses and re-use them to put over your shoes when you place them in your case.

When you arrive at your hotel, take the shoes you have travelled in and place one in the safe with your passport and valuables. When it comes to you leaving to return home, you won't want to travel with just one shoe so you'll have to retrieve it from the safe along with your valuables. I used to do this with my uniform shoes to ensure I didn't leave my passport. If I missed my flight and had to go back to the hotel to get my passport I could end up anywhere! So I always made sure I had that shoe in the safe.

Also always pack substantial pyjamas if you're a sleepwalker like me! I once ended up in the corridor of a hotel after sleepwalking wearing just a see-through camisole top and shorts. Thank goodness I was not naked! The click of the hotel door closing behind me woke me up. Luckily there was a guard on the floor who I managed to get the attention of which saved me the embarrassment of going down to reception.

8) Take your own mug and kettle

I'm sorry to reveal this in this book, but it went round as a rumour when I was working long haul that you should never use the kettle in your hotel room as some crew would boil their dirty knickers in there. So as soon as I heard that one I invested in a small travel kettle and that gets taken everywhere with me! I also take my own mug or reusable coffee cup. There have been many horror stories about maids using dirty towels from the previous guests to wash and dry the mugs in your room.

While we're on the topic of not so nice things in hotel rooms, check the minibars too. Gin and vodka miniatures would often be refilled with water making a not so lovely non-alcoholic drink that you might end up having to pay for! The same with water in bottles too. Check the seals as you never know if a previous guest might have been avoiding paying for their drinks and filling up the mineral water in containers with water from the tap which might not be so safe to drink.

9) Put your money in different pockets

When you're out and about in different places, have money in different pockets or even two wallets if you can and always keep a couple of notes in the sole of your shoe.

I did have a terrifying moment travelling in Ghana. The bus that took us from the airport to our hotel was hijacked. The rumour was these locals were retaliating after local ground crew members had been sacked for stealing cans of Coca Cola from the aircraft. They targeted our bus full of BA staff at a traffic light stop at night. The bus driver took off, and the hijackers got on board with machetes. They smashed the windows of the bus and demanded money and watches from us, one of the crew at the front threw his watch at them. I was luckily at the back of the bus and managed to wedge myself down between the seats. It all happened so fast, but it was terrifying. We were fortunate, and the perpetrators were scared off by cars alongside honking their horns. If you have money in different pockets, this can ensure if you do find yourself in a terrifying situation, you can hand over some cash but not all. Some cabin crew who I worked with even had a fake wallet or purse that they would hand over and keep their valuables on their person in a money belt. Be wary as thieves work in a team, you'd get the one who would squirt you with ketchup or mustard and the other appearing like a kind local offering tissues to help you clean up, they would be the one stealing your purse or wallet!

10) Make friends

Even though the bus hijack was a terrifying experience, it is one small negative encounter in hundreds of positive ones I experienced. It did not stop me from making the most in the cities and places I visited.

Most people are kind and helpful. Most people are not out to get you. Most people will offer advice and guidance if you need it. Most people use the maps on their iPhones, but if you're someone who prefers a paper map, quite often the concierge of a hotel will give you one. Use it discreetly, maybe even behind a local newspaper. I remember being in New York and someone passed and said "bloody tourists" or words to that effect, and I thought how does he know we are tourists as we stood looking up at the skyscrapers mouths agape! So don't be afraid to communicate with local people when travelling, even if there is a language barrier. The universal language of smiling and mime can be quite endearing, and you meet some brilliant people along the way.

When is your next trip? Take this chapter as a sign to get somewhere booked and expand your mind, broaden your horizons and get caught in the buzz and energy of a new adventure.

Part 2 - Expand Your Horizons by Reading and Learning

On New Year's Day 2016, I started a challenge that changed my life. At that point in my then 45 years, I had always felt somewhat cheated out of a real chance of education. My school days were not the happiest, and I felt like I wasn't supported to learn by my teachers.

My job flying all over the world has expanded my horizons in terms of culture and knowledge that still assists me to this day. I love how much of a varied life I have had and the lessons I have picked up from the people, places and cultures I have had the fortunate pleasure of experiencing. I'm told that I am an interesting person to have a conversation with and I credit my continued curiosity for that.

My career in the airline industry has shaped my thirst for knowledge. When I worked as a cabin crew member, life was all about disjointed time zones and broken sleep. People often ask how do you get used to the jet-lag, my answer is you just get used to managing it your way, and everyone was different. For me fresh air on arrival, lots of water and if you can walk barefoot on the grass somewhere even better. I wasn't one for taking any kind of sleep medication but knew many people who took tablets to sleep then tablets to stay awake. It meant there were fun times, partying and jaunting around the globe all hours of day and night but there were difficult times too.

Almost a decade after finishing my career with British Airways, I realised on one sleepy day after Christmas that I had not been learning a tremendous amount of anything new for a while. I wanted to read more again and set myself a goal to do just that. I didn't have the same New Year's Resolutions as many women of my age. I wasn't setting a weight loss goal, doing Dry January or joining a slimming club. I decided I was going to try and consume 100 books over the course of the year. After all, reading is to the mind what exercise is to the body.

What initially started with a list of just a couple of books, soon became a full-on challenge. I should tell you at this point that I had not read a book in YEARS. I mean years. I knew I wanted to read more. I was desperate to continue to learn, expand my mind and find out new things, so me being me, I thought "This is silly, I will never keep at this unless there is a challenge!" so set myself a goal of reading or listening to 100 books in a year.

It had to be either business-related, motivational or inspirational as I am not a fiction fan. (Sorry 50 Shades of Grey you didn't make the cut!) I am also a complete documentary freak and love watching anything adventure related with my friend Keith Partridge or adventurer Steve Backshall. I also absolutely adore David Attenborough and his knowledge of the natural world. I think I might have a little bit of a crush going on there. So knowing what type of books I wanted to read, I created a short wish list of a few books I wanted to tackle via audiobook or paperback. I let my intuition and the recommendation of others guide me to complete the full list of 100 books across the year. In the books, there would be a mention of other titles, so the list grew. I've just finished Becoming Supernatural by Dr Joe Dispenza, and I'm currently starting The Power of Kabbalah. I don't loan out books because, by the time they leave my hands they are not fit for purpose with notes and scribbles, top corner marking my page and the bottom corner is the page with a book recommendation.

I realised I would need to read just shy of two books a week to complete the challenge so I would listen to audiobooks while I was working on tasks that did not require my logical thinking and I would read paperbacks for relaxation purposes at home. I love the feel and smell of a paperback book. I spend a lot of money every month on books but see it as an investment in myself.

Within a couple of months, I noticed a difference in me. I was learning, and I loved it. I felt like I had more time. I stopped consuming as much social media, news and mindless TV. My brain expanded! I could now remember peoples' names easily, recall places and times better too. It was a fascinating experiment with the unexpected but welcome and added bonus of expanded brain function.

The gift of reading was something I wanted to give my son. At the time of writing, he has just turned 12 and has read over 40 books in five months. This makes me proud of his love of learning, but I know it also makes him interesting. His vocabulary is far more extensive than mine. He attended a baby signing group when he was eight months. Baby sign language has been designed to enable babies to communicate before their speech develops. He 'signed' his first word 'rainbow' when he was nine months. Archie never had the terrible 2's or threes for which I hold the additional communication skills accountable. He loves to learn now and takes so much from the stories and fiction books that he loves to read.

The process of reading 100 books in a year was so powerful and mind-blowing that this year I decided to emulate the challenge once again. During the pandemic, my love of reading has helped settle anxiety, and I have enjoyed the escape through a book during the lockdown.

The overriding message I took away from reading my 100 books in a year is that **anything is possible**.

If you set a goal or set yourself a challenge and you stick by it, then you can do it! You should focus on baby steps as they all lead in the right direction to tremendous results. You know that success is not going to happen overnight and so you have to put the work in to get better, learn more, build confidence and thrive in your business. If you focus on pushing yourself out of your comfort zone every day and getting 1 per cent better, you will do it with consistency, and you will get to your goal.

I see too many new business owners wanting to be at a position where they have a ready-made business that is working and profitable. However, the entrepreneur journey doesn't work like that. Success is sequential; you have to put in the work and take those baby steps to see results. You MUST do the groundwork to build your business and expanding your understanding, knowledge, and expertise is crucial for being a success.

I am looking forward to completing my second 100 books in a year challenge as I know it will help me grow as a person and help my business.

Tips for reading more in your day to day life

Audible - is the audiobook subscription app provided by Amazon. If you have never listened to an audiobook, you are missing out! Audible is a fabulous tool, and I love having my favourite books and authors at a click of a button everywhere I go. I listen to audiobooks at any opportunity. Top tip for Audible - you can select the reader speed when you listen so if you select it to x1.5 or x2 you can get through the books faster without it affecting your enjoyment of the content. On the flip side, you can also use the reader speed when listening to Grant Cardone to slow him down!

Language books - I also have Language books on my Audible app so I can scoop a few hours a week on those. I achieved a distinction in Japanese and regularly listen to Spanish and have just taken up Mandarin just because I think "why not".

Create a reading corner or space in your home - make reading a real treat and indulgence. It might be that you read in the bath, or bed or a cosy corner of your home. Dress it up in luscious textiles and fabrics with lots of pillows and comfy throws. You will be itching to retreat to your reading corner at every opportunity.

Set yourself a challenge - no, you don't need to read 100 books in a year like me, but you could set yourself a challenge to read ten pages of a book every day. That way you would read, on average, a book a month. What could you learn from 12 extra books a year? Use the App Madreader for keeping track of your titles. You will get to the stage of not knowing which books you have read. My 50th birthday gift to myself is to purchase 50 books - I'd love to hear your recommendations, please email me jo@jomacfarlane.com.

Read books from experts in your business field - one of the reasons I love non-fiction books and autobiographical books so much is that successful people who publish a book have been there, done it, got the t-shirt. You now have the blueprint in your hands of what they did to make it and make it big. You can learn a lot from your peers and idols.

Read books which will help you learn to be more productive or expand your mindset - to be a thriving entrepreneur; you must wear many hats and juggle many responsibilities. There are so many books out there for time management, productivity, mindset and all aspects of business success. Read what you need, try out the methods and see if you can work smarter and better with the strategies you learn in books.

Ask for recommendations - ask people you know for recommendations of books that have changed their life or taught them valuable lessons. Put a post out on social media asking for recommendations and create your wish list on Amazon of books you've been recommended that you could purchase in the future. As you also listen to audiobooks and read other books, authors will often mention other books that have inspired them, which helps you generate a wider reading wish list.

Turn your car into a University - On the school run after I have dropped off Archie, I get 15 minutes and 15 on the way to pick up, that's 5 hours listening time a month. It was famous speaker Jim Rohn that said: "Turn your car into a University", and that is precisely what I did. I was on a business accelerator program a couple of years ago which was an hour away; I listened to audiobooks every time I drove to and from the programme, and I would also use my language audiobooks too.

Be prepared to read everywhere - I always have a book in my bag and earphones. It makes standing in a queue worthwhile, never again have I complained about waiting. I almost love it! Ten minutes to immerse myself in more 'brain food'.

Collect quotes and things of value - when reading so much you will come across some amazing quotes and nuggets of information that teach you, inspire you or make you feel great. When I am listening to audiobooks, if something of note is said, I will often pause the recording and find a safe place to pull up so I can make a note of what was said and at what time. I make notes in books and also collect   quotes.

100 Books in a Year Challenge 2016 - My Top 3

You can download my 100 books PDF from my website at

www.jomacfarlane.com and see for yourself the kinds of books I consumed over the course of the year. Lots of people now ask me for my recommendations which is why I popped them all onto an easy to download the list for anyone keen to take up a reading challenge too.

From my original 2015-16 challenge, if I had to pick the books that were my top three from my full list, they would be:

- Think & Grow Rich by Napoleon Hill
- Eat that Frog by Brian Tracy
- The Miracle Morning by Hal Elrod

Part 3 - Expand Your Horizons through your Connections

'The more you talk, the more you find out about people.'

Expanding your horizons through your connections and your social circle does not just mean face to face; it means online too. I love getting to know people and talking in person and online, forging friendships and professional relationships and expanding my network.

When you connect with others, always remember the rule that we are all connected by seven degrees of separation. Be kind, polite and listen to others so you leave a good impression and they remember you. This includes social media. What are you known for? What do you want to be known for? This goes back to your values exercise, and it helps you find your voice on social media to promote yourself or your business.

When networking face to face at business events, take a genuine interest in people. You may have heard of an elevator pitch where you sum up what you do in one sentence. This is the short response you give when someone asks who you are and what you do at these events. You want to be memorable and stand out. This is a great way to strike up interesting conversations, but it also helps people to remember you and what you do. Gemma, my writing partner on this book, once worked in a PR agency and her elevator pitch was "I make people famous." Short and sweet, but it meant people were engaged and wanted to know more. What she actually meant was that she would secure PR coverage, award entries and TV/Radio appearances for her clients, therefore making them 'famous' in their industries and sectors.

I have to admit, over recent years, I have not done much face to face networking, but there is still a place for it in bricks and mortar businesses. Having a genuine connection face to face with people builds trust and rapport, and getting out there talking about your business helps you shout about what you do and how great you are at it. When you first start going to networking events, it can feel daunting, and you don't know what to say. Sometimes, listening is more powerful than talking. People generally love to talk about themselves and their achievements, and you can learn a lot about people from what they say in these situations.

There are also many online spaces to network in dedicated business clubs and groups on social media. Not everyone is who they say they are online, though, and it is wise to be cautious and wary if striking up a conversation does not feel right, and you are not aligned.

There are many paid memberships online that can help you connect with other like-minded entrepreneurs or learn and be mentored in a group of people in your sector. I am a member of Enterprise Nation, Lightbulb and The Social Sales Girls as well as non paid groups. Women regularly converse in that group and connect on a range of shared business topics. There is always someone in there sharing a story that is inspirational, motivational and helps you learn something new. I run my own small Facebook group for those people looking to get into candle making. It is a great space where a small group of candle enthusiasts can learn from one another, connect and share their business experiences. I have faced criticism in the past for sharing my candle making secrets and hosting a group like this as these members could become 'competition' however I have the firm belief that there is enough for all of us and collaboration is better and more powerful than competition.

I enter award entries for my business for two reasons. 1) the business deserves to win! 2) it is a great opportunity to raise the profile of the business and also meet other people and expand my connections. I have been fortunate to be named in the Small Business 100 with Theo Paphitis and have showcased my candles in Downing Street. I have attended events at The House of Lords and created candles for the event there and won awards in different categories across the UK. Attending these awards has been powerful for me, both on a personal and professional level (nothing like the feeling of a trophy in your hand!) but I have also met some amazing people who have genuinely shaped the course of my life. I met my book writing co-author Gemma, who I mentioned earlier, through a connection made at The Small Awards. A lady called Claire Moore had been nominated after her business won Ladies Gym of the Year at the National Fitness Awards. We sat on the same table but not together. In fact, we had to shout a bit to talk to one another and connect. Claire said, "I'm only here because of Gemma who writes my awards." At the time, I had been struggling with award entry writing and had been wondering who I could call on to help. I took Gemma's details, and a few weeks later we were working together on some more award entries. We clicked straight away, shared values and interests, and even after the award entries were done, we stayed in touch. Gemma had written her own books so a few months later, when I was looking to write my own, I reached out to Gemma to see if she knew anyone who could help me publish my book. It turns out Gemma had changed careers and was now helping would-be writers with their books. I didn't expect that I contacted her to ask for her advice and ended up with a writing coach to help me publish this book. If I'd stayed quiet at the Small Awards and not bothered to take the time to talk to Claire, I would not have known about Gemma, and you would not be reading these very words right now.

I love moments like that in life. I call them Sliding Doors moments after the film with Gwyneth Paltrow. Do you remember that one? Where the film plays two versions of her life out: one where she gets on the tube and goes home to a shock and another where she misses the tube, the sliding doors shut and her life takes a very different turn. I love looking back on those moments and the connections I have made and realising that they shaped and changed my life in some way.

When I was accepted for an interview for British Midland, I was flown to the interview from Edinburgh to Heathrow. Upon boarding the flight, I got talking to this lovely Australian flight attendant Tim who noticed that I was on a free flight from the boarding list. I told him I was going for an interview and we got talking. He asked me what airport I wanted to work out of and I said "Edinburgh". "Have you not considered Heathrow?" he asked, explaining more about the routes and layovers. At that point, I hadn't thought it was possible. I just thought Edinburgh would be the only option! Had I not spoken to him, I may have said no to the subsequent job offer that came. Instead, I ended up working out of Heathrow, which later led me to work for British Airways. I am a firm believer I was meant to have that conversation. The Universe put us together at that moment to steer my path.

You just never know who knows who, and who can help you, which is why I always take the time to strike up conversations and connect with new people. Expanding my connections and learning to be open to new opportunities and new people has been part and parcel of my entrepreneurial life. I strongly advise you to do the same, even if you're a natural introvert, even if it feels scary. Get yourself out there and let people know who you are and what you're offering the world!

Don't be frightened to go alone to events. I think you have more chance of effective networking when you're alone. When you go with someone else, you end up hanging out together. Whereas when you're on your own, you have no choice but to connect with others. I had the opportunity to go to Tony Robbins' event in London and almost took my husband. In the end, I went on my own, and I was so glad!

When I was still travelling to the States every week as a flight attendant, I would watch Tony Robbins on TV, mesmerised. This loud, high energy, almost 7-foot 'god' almost preached on these infomercials. I had never seen anything like him, coming from a tiny fishing village on the East Coast of Scotland with only 2000 inhabitants, there was nobody like Tony in my life. All I knew was I needed what he was on; I ordered the CDs that he was advertising on the infomercial.

I couldn't wait for his CDs to arrive. When they did, I devoured them; I played them over and over in the car. I still have them to this day. I had a meeting with a friend who said they were going to go and see him live. "Whaaat? Where? But I'm the Tony Robbins fan, how come I haven't heard about this?!" A few minutes later my email pinged - Tony Robbins was coming to London! Stop the bus! This I was not going to miss, but wait - it was a firewalk event! All the better, Tony Robbins to hold my hand while walking on 1000 degree hot coals.

Of course, Tony didn't personally hold my hand, but what an experience. It was a weekend of mind-blowing information and testing times. My brain was full, and I loved every second, I couldn't get enough, not forgetting the high octane jumping around, high fiving and hugging complete strangers.

We worked with our Fire Walk partner for a good few hours; we were going to support each other over the coals by keeping each other in 'the zone' then a twist was announced. Turn to the person on your left, now that person has just become your partner. The weekend was filled with activities that pushed me into, and well beyond my comfort zone, I didn't know whether to run for the door or enjoy it.

I met some fantastic people at that event who challenged my ideas and beliefs. I met my coach Jacob there and also got talking to the most interesting people. I would not have had the same experience had I gone with my husband or friends. This pushed me out of my comfort zone and was a great experience. I am planning to take my son to see Tony Robbins for his 18th birthday instead of the standard 'go to the pub' event when he comes of age.

The other great thing that came out of going to see Tony Robbins was that I started up with a mindset coach. I think it's important to have a coach in life, someone who has trod the path before you. You don't know what you don't know, and they know it! You might want to look for a coach to help you achieve your goals in sport, improve your skills, gain motivation or achieve a specific business goal. That's why I love coaching other small business owners on my Ignite Your Creativity course. I get to guide them through the pitfalls and the highs that I have experienced on my journey.

You don't always find great connections within your niche. I'd encourage you to reach out and look wider to find new business connections. If there were someone I wanted to be my mentor, I would just be brave and ask. Remember, people are human and asking is a great skill. Don't be scared to ask! If you want to connect with new people, start by taking your connection offline where possible and have a good old fashioned conversation. You can carry a conversation by email, but it's not until you hear someone that you get a true sense of connection. Always make sure you smile when you are chatting too and always be yourself, "everyone else is taken", or so the story goes. Always consider ways you can help that person, not the other way around. Don't be all take take take in business, that isn't how it works.

Connecting digitally is so easy in today's world. I have worked with freelance people in the States, the Middle East and Africa. Don't limit who you work with by their country of residence; I find tapping into people who live in a different cultural environment exciting. Ask a mutual friend to connect you if you see there is a common ground.

Be persistent; I'd at least try seven times to connect with someone, you can land in someone's spam, they can open it at an inconvenient time, they may be on holiday and a lot of the time people are genuinely glad you messaged back. I know I am glad when people are consistent and end up working with people that stay in the front of your mind. There is an old American proverb - "The squeaky wheel gets the grease" the person who makes the most noise gets noticed.

Linkedin is a great way to connect. If you are looking to have work featured in a publication cast your net wide, research the media and connect, send a personal note to let people know why you are connecting.
"Connection is the energy that is created between people when they feel seen, heard and valued." Brene Brown

Be open to any connections no matter how obscure they may appear, I am very serendipitous (one who finds valuable or agreeable things not sought for) and open and trust the universe to send who is right for me at that time.

Make a list here of who you would like to be connected to, put it out there and watch and be open to opportunities that will link you.

1.
2.
3.

Chapter 3

Feel Good

"If you feel good, you're going to look good."

- Julia Jones

Dress Well

I adore dressing well. I think this has been unshakeable within me since my cabin crew days where uniform regulations were super strict. From stiffly starched shirts to immaculate not-a-hair-out-of-place coiffed hairstyles and the regulation lipstick, I lived and breathed dressing well for over a decade.

I always feel that it is better to be overdressed than underdressed. I think you're more likely to feel uncomfortable if you haven't dressed for the occasion. It isn't just my own experience of dressing well. Countless scientific studies have been conducted in the psychology of dressing up and dressing well.

We have been conditioned by our culture to perceive those we deem as attractive as more favourable subconsciously. Studies show that attractive people are considered to be more successful and also more sociable and happy. In the 1972 'What is Beautiful is Good' a study by Karen Dion and Ellen Berscheid of the University of Minnesota and Elaine Walster of The University of Wisconsin, the scientists tested whether a person's appearance and attractiveness influenced the judgement of others. The study determined that both attractive men and women were assumed to possess more socially desirable personality traits and were expected to lead better lives (e.g. be more compatible partners, more trustworthy, be more successful occupationally) than those subjects deemed unattractive.

In one study, attractive people are said to make around an average of $230,000 more throughout their professional earning lifetime. In psychological tests, women who wear makeup were perceived as more competent, likeable and trustworthy. Study participants were shown faces for .25 seconds and asked them to rate the photographs of the study subjects on competence, likability, attractiveness and trustworthiness. A 'glamorous' face with full makeup rated highest on every category.

Interestingly, more studies suggest that you can improve your physical attractiveness by improving your clothing attractiveness. In 2009, the Home Economics Research Journal tested the influence of clothing on attractiveness. They asked those participating in the study to rate the competence, work comfort and sociability of six different models. Three models wore clothing deemed to be attractive, while the remaining three models wore clothing considered unattractive and scruffy. The result of the study showed that models in attractive clothing were perceived much more positively than those in the unattractive clothing. As a result, researchers concluded that "clothing attractiveness" can have a similar positive effect as actual physical attractiveness.

I am not here to preach and tell everyone to wear makeup and dress well. Yes, I can share study findings and statistics, but it is about how you feel on the inside and out. It is about the power of fashion, beauty and your health for you as an individual. Some people never feel ready for the day without a face of makeup while others prefer to focus on their natural selves. There is no right or wrong answer with this. It is about personal choice although Oscar Wilde did famously state that "You can never be overdressed or overeducated".

Personally, I wouldn't put the bin out without a full face of makeup on! If I'm running at 5 am, and it is pitch black outside, even if I know the run is going to finish in pitch black I still put my makeup on. I'm always selfie-ready or always with my face on incase I bump into someone I know - even at 5 am! My makeup is applied whatever the weather and the occasion. Even when I was swimming in the sea every day, my waterproof mascara was on, and my eyebrows were shaded in. My friend who I ran the New York marathon with couldn't believe the staying power of my face and was like "Oh my god you've just run a marathon, and your makeup is still intact!" Although that might be due to the fact I wasn't exerting myself too much!

It goes back to my long haul days where I would wear makeup that felt an inch thick and apply my lipstick with precision multiple times per flight. My lipstick would even be flawless at 3 am! When you face such strict regulations and rules around your appearance, it becomes difficult to shake off, even in the 12 years since I left the world of long haul flying.

I would wear regulation tights, regulation hairpins and bobbles, regulation shoes. Every aspect of my appearance was closely monitored and controlled. Yet with the scrutiny came a certain sense of routine. I always knew what to wear and how to present myself. In the same way, Mark Zuckerberg from Facebook and Simon Cowell wear the same outfits daily, it takes away the decision fatigue of what to wear when you know exactly what it is you will be wearing every day.

When you start your own business, as you may be doing having picked up this book, what to wear crops up a lot in conversation, there's a lot of jokes made online that working from home means you can work from your pyjamas. It is understandable if you've escaped a rigid 9-5 or a job where you've been used to wearing a uniform or strict corporate dress. However, the most significant piece of advice I can give you as an entrepreneur and someone who has built a business from my kitchen table is number one rule - never ever ever work in your pyjamas. It's my greatest non-negotiable "no".

Finding My Colour

I have my own definite style when it comes to clothing. I have always opted for neutral colours and always gravitated towards the darker colours.

I like structured and fitted clothing. A well-cut pair of black trousers and cashmere polo neck or a crisp white shirt by Land's End would be my outfit of choice paired with stylish flats or boots in the winter. I can't stand anything floaty or floral except in nightwear. I think psychologically for me wearing loose floaty clothes makes me feel loose and floaty. I'm also somewhat averse to colour.

A few years ago I went to the Best You Expo with a friend. I saw The Colour Ministry stand (thecolourministry.co.uk) and Alison, who runs the organisation, stood there surrounded by rainbow colours. The stand was full, and Alison was explaining how her company of professional colour consultants helped individuals and businesses find the colours for them. I didn't go to the stand - I am allergic to colour! So we just walked past, and I didn't think anything of it.

That night after the Expo we went out for dinner and got chatting to a couple of people on the table next to us who had also been at the Expo. They started raving about Alison and The Colour Ministry and insisted that I must go and see her early before the crowds arrived. The next morning I headed straight to her stand. She was just setting up. We ended up chatting over coffee, and it was the most fantastic experience. I gave Alison my date of birth, and she was able to tell me all sorts about my life without being prompted. It was truly extraordinary. We spoke for over an hour, and she was so interesting. Alison suggested that my natural colour for my personality, aura and energy field should be red but saw my shock as I recoiled at the thought of wearing something so bright and garish. I am a dark and black clothing girl through and through. It would take a miracle for me to ditch the familiar and wear red.

Alison suggested that my bright energy might be overpowering for some, so my wearing darker colours was a subconscious way to mute that. Still intent on me embracing my natural red coloured self, she suggested I get some red underwear and start eating red foods. My husband Stuart thought I had gone mad for buying red underwear, knowing not a stitch of colour is in my wardrobe, and I did feel acutely aware of it every time I put it on! Wearing red is supposed to connect me to my root chakra and is a reminder of who I am at my core. I just hope I don't get run over and they have to cut my clothing off revealing the racy red knickers!

You Can't Trust a Skirt!

I don't tend to wear skirts and especially not long skirts. This dates back to a mortifying experience when I spent a few short months working at an advertising agency. This was before my cabin crew days, but I was still intent on dressing well. This particular day I'd worn a super stylish long skirt with tights and heels. I felt fantastic and very confident in my fashion choices.

I was called to the office to have a meeting with the big boss. On arrival, he wasn't quite ready for me, so I used the short delay to head to the ladies and use the mirrors to check my appearance. Sadly there wasn't a full-length mirror that revealed my error. I walked from the ladies to the meeting and as I stood up to leave and turned to the door my boss coughed and said "Ah-hem, Jo you er, might want to er…" and pointed up and down with a very very red face towards my derriere. There, tucked into the back of my knickers was my long stylish skirt revealing my underwear, stockings and backside to my poor boss.

Truly one of the most humiliating and embarrassing moments of my whole life! It is no wonder a skirt rarely features in my clothing these days. You can't trust a skirt!

Get "Dressed to the Shoes"

There is a woman I follow called The Fly Lady. You can catch her content online at www.theflylady.net, and we are lucky that my local community magazine, The Edition, runs a column by The Fly Lady. She is like the original Mrs Hinch or The Organised Mum (if you follow these popular ladies online), but she is also wise and full of the most amazing life hacks to make you feel fantastic. The Fly Lady has been publishing her top tips on all things home and lifestyle for almost 20 years and has a substantial international following.

The Fly Lady says "getting dressed to shoes" is one of her most essential life tips because when you've got your shoes on, you've got your clothes on, you're ready to work and get some things done. FlyLady believes that you act and feel differently when you are completely dressed with shoes on your feet - even if you are not leaving the house. It makes you feel ready to go! I remember reading this myself a few years ago, and it resonated with me. I started to get "dressed to the shoes", and I do this in a big way every single day.

There's a brilliant story on the Fly Lady website where she talks about the time she worked at a direct sales cosmetics company. One main rule for the company was that you were not allowed to make a single phone call in the morning until you were fully dressed, including dressed in your shoes. The reason behind this was that the company believed you think and act differently when you have clothes and shoes on. You are more professional. The customer can tell if you don't feel good about the way you look - even down the phone. So if getting dressed makes that much of an impression on those that cannot see you, how big of an impact will you make to those that can see you? The Fly Lady even takes it one step further and suggests that those who work from home or work for their own business should wear lace-up shoes rather than slip-on or sandals as you can't just kick your shoes off for a quick nap on the sofa. With shoes on your feet, your mind says "OK, it's time to go to work." And you're less likely to procrastinate.

This is often the case for stay at home mums, or those parents creating a side hustle business from home. It's why in my Ignite Your Creativity 12-week course that sees you go from idea to launched business, I tell all my students whether they're stay-at-home parents or not to "Get dressed to the shoes." It ensures you get dressed every morning, and you feel like you have a purpose. Even if your children are going to be the only people to see you during the day (especially if you're following my 5-9, 9-5. 5-9 MethodTM which we will talk about later), wearing shoes will literally keep you on your toes and keep you feeling productive.

"But I don't wear shoes in the house!" You may say. Well, you do now! Buy a pair or clean up a pair you don't wear outside and get some lace-up heels if possible. Lace them up and wear them tall and proud in the house. You will be utterly amazed at how different you feel.

When I do coaching calls with my students on the Ignite Your Creativity course, even if they are not video calls, I still wear my heels, and I still stand up. It completely changes my energy and posture. It makes me feel different to my core. It is too easy to get complacent in the way you dress when you work from home, so get those shoes on and send those signals to your brain that you are ready and prepared for anything.

Try it for a week. Make a pledge to yourself that you will dress in stylish clothes, put on your makeup and wear nice shoes in the house while you are working. Do this for a working week - Monday to Friday, and see how you feel in yourself, your productivity levels and your confidence. I assure you it will make you feel different. Even if you're sat typing at your desk, get your sassiest shoes on with your stylish clothes, and you'll ooze more self-esteem.

Shine Your Shoes

OK, so we've learned about the power of wearing shoes. Another of my top tips is shining your shoes! I never leave home without a mini shoe shining kit in my handbag.

When writing out this book, I wondered if I would come across as ludicrous for carrying a shoeshine and mini polish. It is just something that was passed onto me from my father and his Merchant Navy days. He would shine my school shoes for me, and I have passed this onto my son. Every morning he shines his shoes before school. They come back covered in scuff and mud, but every day he starts the day as he means to go on - looking his best. When he was just six years old in primary school, the children were given an option of which school uniform to wear. They could choose school trousers and a polo shirt or shirt and tie. My son decided to wear a shirt and tie each day and was the only child in his class to do so. I was worried he might look like the odd one out and get picked on, but he insisted, and for the next five years of his school life he continued to wear and shirt and tie each day.

I must admit it makes me very proud but going back to the psychology and studies behind dress, men who dress well are more likely to get a job after being interviewed, and their job performances tend to be rated higher. In a study by Men's Health magazine and

Opinion Research Corporation, more than 1,000 women were surveyed on the traits they find most attractive in a man. They ranked 'his sense of style' as the most important physical attribute of a man. This ranked higher than a handsome face, muscular build, height and even fitness, which means that a sense of style, something entirely within everyone's control is the most important physical trait to make a man attractive to women. So what happens when someone is deemed more attractive, employable, trustworthy? They have it a little easier, which is why I've always let my son find his sense of style, but I'm secretly thrilled that he also loves to dress well.

Starting with shining your shoes mighty seem petty or anal, but it again relates to your subconscious. As you look at your shoes, and you can see they are well presented and shiny, it makes you feel a sense of pride in yourself. If you have ever headed out with clothes that are not ironed and very creased, you may have felt that pang of self-conscious uncomfortableness. I think that dirty shoes evoke that same feeling as clothes that have not been ironed. It is all about stepping out with confidence every day. That's why every day I step into a pair of shined and polished shoes.

Dressing Well Does Not Have to Cost the Earth (It Might Just Save It Though!)

In 2019 I pledged that I would not buy any new clothing for the whole year. Anything I would buy in 2019 would be pre-loved from websites like eBay or charity shops.

I had been to a climate change demonstration with my son in 2018 and decided that we all needed to start playing our part as a family. I made changes in my business with materials and recyclables, we made changes to our household purchases as a family and looked at how we could be more sustainable.

One area that always concerned me from an environmental and ethical point of view was fast fashion. I love clothes. I always have done. I love to dress well and have a particular personal brand and style when it comes to clothes.

So deciding to stop indulging in the pastime I love was a shock for many in my immediate circle. I didn't stop shopping, I just changed where I shopped, and it was a wonderful, valuable year of self-discovery and sustainability.

Initially, I thought this challenge would be hard. I envisaged myself going a bit wild on January 1st as the challenge came to an end and splurging on all new clothing. However, the year of buying nothing new taught me so much about myself, about the society we live in, about sustainable fashion, about saving money and about style.

In my year of buying nothing new, I had some very important events to attend, including a lunch at the House of Lords. The invitation said 'Business Dress' so I asked my social media followers to help me pick the perfect outfit. I showcased a navy dress, a peach InWear designer dress and a cream dress—all charity shop purchases. My followers decided that the peach dress had to be the one, so I paired it with a beautiful MaxMara jacket and Stuart Weitzman for Russel and Bromley shoes that were £1.70 in a charity shop in the Highlands. The whole outfit cost less than £20. I strutted into The House of Lords feeling super confident if a little out of my comfort zone as I'd usually be in black clothing. This time though everyone else was wearing black and grey. So actually, my colourful outfit stood out, and I was noticed. This helped me network and meet new and exciting people.

I have found an absolute treasure trove of charity shops in Edinburgh, and it is a real treat for me heading there to find new and thrilling purchases. I always like to put it out to the Universe before I head there and ask for what I'm looking for. "Ski jacket for Archie, winter coat and leather boots today please!" I might say looking up to the sky. I usually find everything I am looking for and more. I couldn't believe how easy it was to find a ski jacket! Archie was heading on a ski trip, and as a growing boy, I didn't want to shell out hundreds of pounds for something that would get worn once. I was delighted to pick up a perfect ski jacket that looked almost new for around £5. I also found myself drawn to a Duvetica jacket. I hadn't heard of the brand before, but it was waist length, super warm and had the most adorable fake fur hood. I loved that jacket and picked it up for around £4.50. I was wearing it in Harvey Nichols and couldn't believe that they stocked the full and new range there. £450 for a brand new jacket and here I was in mine at a hundredth of the price!

I've found some fabulous pieces including a pair of bronze Manolo Blahnik sandals. I wore them around the house a few times before admitting defeat and realising they didn't fit properly. They looked gorgeous on display in my bedroom before I parted ways and sold them on eBay. I also one day had ten minutes to spare before a networking meeting. The shoes I was wearing were a little uncomfortable, and I noticed a charity shop close by. I put it out to the Universe that I needed some new stylish but comfortable shoes and couldn't believe it when pumps of one of my favourite designers, Tory Burch, were on sale! They were my size, wine-coloured and featured the gold Tory Burch emblem (I have the earrings to match). These pumps were £250 new, but I grabbed them for the unbelievable price of £6.

I also found some amazing clothes in London in charity shops. The prices are more expensive, but Mary Portas Living & Giving charity shop in Primrose Hill was spectacular and full of designer and unique pieces. I was in heaven! Charity shops in Edinburgh are amazing. You can get designer gear for a fraction of the price. The fashion brand Cos donate a lot of their surplus and sample clothing to the British Heart Foundation in Edinburgh, so it is a great shop to pick up some exceptional pieces. The Morningside area of Edinburgh is also a treasure trove of pre-loved goods. They said the ladies of Morningside of old were "all fur coat and no knickers" meaning they'd pay a fortune for their fur coat but go without the knickers. They wanted to be seen as really affluent with the fur coat and so couldn't afford their undergarments. These shops carry the affluence of Morningside and the items I find there are often special and stunning.

I do pick up many different pieces and sometimes batch shop for the future. As I mentioned Mark Zuckerberg and Simon Cowell wearing the same things over and over as it saves brain space, I do the same for important events. If I see cocktail dresses or designed dresses that would be perfect for events, awards ceremonies and weddings, I pick them up. I got three dresses in my size from Reiss for £4.99 each recently and earmarked each one for a wedding, event or upcoming party. It means that when these events and parties come around in the diary, I am ready with something to wear. I don't have to go stress shopping for the right outfit when I have one to hand. I've usually got shoes and a bag to match too, so I am ready for anything. I will also always take a second outfit to any event just in case. I'll always carry spare tights, spare flat pumps and that all-important shoe shine whenever I am heading somewhere important.

I tend to indulge a little more with my charity shop shopping sprees. As prices are so low, I have an excuse to buy regularly without the guilt. I have friends who won't even step foot in a charity shop, but I think it is important for us to be mindful of the clothes we wear and the impact it can have when they end up in landfill. I have tried to campaign for a second-hand charity room attached to my son's old school, but this was not met positively by some of the parents who place a stigma on second-hand items. His new school has a great 'pre-loved' uniform store where we can also donate barely worn items too, and the kids are very open to it.

I find it such a shame that this stigma exists. Often we will discard clothing when it is still full of life. Just because we are done with it, it doesn't mean that it is ready for the rubbish tip. I often donate our clothes to charity shops to continue the cycle. Fast fashion is being produced on a mass scale unethically and very cheaply. This has an environmental impact at the point of manufacture and also at the point where these cheaply made items are discarded and sent to landfill. The organic cotton t-shirts that the Ignite Your Creativity tribe receive when they finish their course are from Rapanui. They are printed in the UK in a renewable energy powered factory; you can read their amazing story here www.rapanuiclothing.com. The t-shirts are designed to be sent back to the company to be recycled after use and not go into landfill.

My son regularly comes with me to charity shops as I want him also to know there is nothing wrong with wearing pre-loved items. His generation is the one most at risk with climate change, and his generation is waking up to what they can do to play a positive part.

His generation is the one that will make a difference. They are the generation who hold the decisions of the future.

Experiment with Your Own Style

If you do fancy finding your own style and dressing to feel great every single day, then shopping in charity shops is a low-cost way to try new colours and styles on yourself. Head to more affluent areas to seek out more designer clothing or go to different cities and scour vintage shops and preloved boutiques.

If you don't know where to start with your own style, you could utilise the services of a personal shopper to discover who you are when it comes to fashion. Many high street department stores have a free personal shopper service including John Lewis, Topshop and some Next stores. You could even ask retail assistants for their advice at your favourite shop. If they are good and they love their job, they will understand trends and colours and may be able to offer advice. Personal shoppers will assess your body shape and come up with clothing combinations that work for your physique, skin tone and natural colouring. You can even find freelance personal shoppers who can help you with a full consultation service. Often freelance personal shoppers will meet with you over a couple of appointments and may find low-cost alternatives to pieces and styles you pick - making a cost-saving and therefore better return on investment.

As explained earlier in the chapter, you could have your colour profile analysed. Thecolourministry.co.uk connects you to a local consultant, or you can even book an appointment that can be conducted online via Skype. If you don't want to invest in a paid-for service, there are plenty of websites where you can access information and surveys about discovering the right colours for you, for free. It's not just about wearing colour but eating different colours and drinking from different coloured glass too.

Pinterest is an excellent resource for clothing and styles. You can pin your favourite styles and colours and then reference these images when you go out shopping. Try these kinds of outfits and colours on yourself, take a photo in the changing room and compare to the photos you have pinned. There is a great new app by Trupik that lets you create a 3D digital self of your body and see what you look like wearing their clothes making it easier to see what suits you, aimed at bridging the disconnection between online and offline—using a body mapping technique which would usually be used for landscaping. Make sure you go with your makeup and hair done and feeling your best. You always look different when you're made over compared to trying on outfits bare-faced and with your hair scraped back under the harsh changing room lights.

Follow fashionistas on social media. There are some great stylists on Instagram who often operate style challenges. For a month, you are asked to wear certain things every day and hashtag your progress. It is a great way to try out new styles, colours, accessories and connect with others also going through the same process. Look through the #stylechallenge hashtag to see if any monthly styling challenges catch your eye that you could participate in.

Take a girlfriend with you and have a day trying on all different kinds of outfits and styles. Get your friend to tell you what flatters your shape and which colours suit you. Getting a second opinion always helps.

Go through your wardrobes and drawers, Marie Kondo style. Ask yourself which of your items of clothing 'spark joy' and notice a pattern. What colours are you drawn towards? What styles? What do you feel sexy yet comfortable and confident in? What items do people tend to offer you compliments when you wear them? Have a clear out of the items that don't fit or flatter and keep to a capsule wardrobe of items you can mix and match together.

Whatever you wear though remember, always dress to your shoes!

Your Health is Your Wealth

I would say I am very health conscious, and I am always aware of what I am going to put in my body and how I am going to feel after consuming certain foods and drink. I know what makes me function better and what foods give me clarity. I don't think I would have been as successful as I have in business without making my health a priority. Having my health in optimum condition helps me think better, control my emotions better, sleep better and perform better.

What makes you feel good, and what are you not doing that you know will instantly make you feel better? Don't worry about what you haven't been doing. Just focus on right now and start now. You can't undo that entire chocolate bar you ate for lunch yesterday, but you can make a change right now.

A lot of people ask me for my suggestions with health, getting fit and feeling good. These would be my top priorities:

Fresh air - you cannot beat getting out into nature and getting some fresh air. This is so good for your mind and your body. Blue skies and expansive horizons make you feel less cooped up, and a walk in nature is a great way to get in your steps, have your thinking time and get that all-important fresh air.

Breathe deeper - I talk about this in more detail in Chapter 5, Your Ideal Day. I use the Wim Hof method of deep breathing to increase my oxygen intake and reduce inflammation in the body.

Meditation - I am a big fan of meditation and will go into this in more detail in Chapter 5, but meditating allows me to feel like I am resting my brain and getting much clearer on what I want out of my life. It is the most amazing tool I wish I'd known about years ago.

Read - Reading expands your mind and your capacity to learn and grow. Read often via paperback and audiobook. It's always non-fiction titles from the world's greatest thinkers on my reading list.

Dance - I love to dance and used to do ballet up until I was a teenager. I did join an adult ballet group for a while and loved getting back into my dance moves. Dancing switches up your energy and your state. I learned this at Tony Robbins' live event I attended. Moving your body is so powerful to change your mindset and your momentum in a moment.

Gratitude - You might think this isn't something to do with health, but for me, this is one of the most amazing things for my mental health and mental state. I like to write down three things that I am grateful for each morning. When I forget to write it down, I like to think about it and feel into the thanks for whatever it is I am expressing gratitude for.

Tongue scraping - This might sound a little 'out there' but give it a try! I use a copper hoop as copper is supposed to be good for antibacterial purposes. I put it at the back of my mouth and scrape quite lightly. What comes off your tongue is quite revolting, but I like to do this twice a day. Tongue scraping is an ancient Ayurvedic practice that is said to help remove bacteria, improve breath and dental hygiene, eliminate toxins excreted from the body, improve the appearance of the tongue and enhance your taste buds. There are many resources online to look at pictures of your tongue and see if different conditions in your body have manifested on your tongue.

Fasting - This is a relatively new discipline for me, and I started intermittent fasting after missing breakfast a couple of days and realising it helped reduce my cravings throughout the day. After reading various articles about the benefits of having an empty stomach and giving your digestive system a break, I decided to try it myself. The approach of continually filling my stomach with snacks throughout the day never made sense to me, eating first thing in the morning always makes me eat vast amounts during the day. My method of fasting involves avoiding food for 16/18 hours then consuming food for a 6/8 hour window; many believe this supports the body's cell renewal and immune system.

According to science, fasting has been known to boost brain function and prevent neurodegenerative disorders like Parkinson's and dementia. Studies have shown that it also reduces inflammation, according to healthline.com adults taking part in a study reduced their inflammatory markers significantly after fasting for a month. TV Dr and adventurer Michael Mosely reversed his type 2 diabetes and lost 22lbs with intermittent fasting, and he was an inspiration for me taking this path.

If you are thinking of practising fasting, here is what I have personally discovered:

- Don't scoff like a pig at the end of the fast! My stomach couldn't cope. Make sure you break your fast with nutritionally dense foods that your body will thank you for.

- Track your energy throughout and after your fast. You will realise the right timings for you and your fasting journey. You should experience a sense of calm and peace. I used to get a 3 pm slump in the day and fasting has meant this has not happened as much.

- Be grateful for your food. When the fast breaks I am so grateful for the food I am receiving, like never before have I appreciated food so much and I look at it differently. I have most recently tried having lunch at 2 pm and fasting through to 10 am the next day, and that is easier.

- Focus on the benefits. If you get rid of the idea that you are 'doing without' and the benefits of what fasting brings, it's easier. Serotonin (the happy hormone) produced in the gut as well as the brain is essential for many things, including our good mood and it can only be produced when the gut is empty.

I haven't tried dry fasting yet, where you avoid food and any contact with water - you don't even wash (I would have to negotiate this with my son and husband) and you don't brush your teeth. I personally wouldn't try it as I believe water is vital to our daily health. I have found during fasting that mostly I am thirsty and not hungry and get a bit of a headache. I do also find it easier nearer the end of the fast and try to push an extra half or hour in at the end. The part I find the hardest is if I am fasting for 18 hours and my last meal was 6 pm, that means I would break my fast at midday the next day. However, when I wake at 5 am, it means I have 7 hours before I eat and that can be tough! Sometimes it is the thought of having such a long time before I can eat that drives me mad, but if I can be disciplined with my thoughts and put this out of my mind, it becomes easier. I will still prepare soup and food during these times, and it takes willpower not to nibble!

Mental Health

We feed our body but forget that we need to feed our mind and soul too. Your diet is not only what you eat. It's what you watch, what you listen to, what you read, the people you hang around. Be mindful of the things you put into your body emotionally, spiritually and physically.

Keeping yourself in a positive mind frame takes a considerable effort, it might be challenging to begin with, but discipline takes time, and I believe Rome wasn't built in a day. I don't try and change more than a couple of things at a time. I am free to try things daily with no considerable commitment to making it into a challenge. At time of writing, I am on a 365 day Yoga journey (long term goal) lose two stone (medium-term goal) and cut out bread (short term goal) because bread and I have a love-hate relationship, and currently we are on a break while I attempt to try the ketogenic diet. I don't watch trash on TV or consume fiction books.

The language that you use to talk to yourself can have a direct impact on your health. According to a study by Elizabeth Quinn, positive self-talk in sports psychology is one of the hardest things for an athlete to master. Healthy self-talk can have a positive effect on our physical state, so really notice how you talk to yourself daily. Is it positive or negative? Critical or supportive?

Many more ways make you feel good; the next chapter will talk about your immediate personal and business environment and how that can help you feel your best.

Exercise: How Can You feel Good?

After reading this chapter, think about what has come up for you in terms of feeling good.

1. What do you currently do that makes you feel good?

2. What do you currently do that makes you feel foggy?

3. What three tiny changes could you commit to that will help you feel good in your body, brain and business?

Chapter 4

Create Your Environment

"Arrange your personal space to support the way you work and live."

- Jeff Davidson

I am a massive lover of Feng Shui. I read a book about it over 30 years ago and combined with my travel to the Far East; I've been a devotee ever since. When you create the space, mentally and physically, for new things, your energy and creativity will increase. Feng Shui in your life and business is about understanding the flow of energy and embracing the joy of removing physical and mental clutter from your life. I think Feng Shui is so much more than about money or interior design; for me, it forms a fundamental part of my home and working environments that brings great joy and comfort. The notion that it brings money I believe comes from being in a space where the energy is right for productivity, creation and entrepreneurship. That's where the return on investment comes in. When your energy is right, everything feels easier.

This chapter is all about creating your environment and works in three parts for me; your home environment, your working environment, the wider ecological environment and the role we play in ensuring that thrives.

Your Home Environment

Now you might be wondering what impact your home environment may have on your business. I would say it is everything. Having your home set up in a way that supports your well-being will make you happier, less stressed, more creative, more settled and create the perfect haven from which to retreat from work. Thinking of another ancient Chinese philosophy, Yin and Yang, you must have the right space and environment at home in order to flourish at work. The two are opposites, but they feed into each other and complement one another too.

When I first started my candle making business, I started it from my kitchen table. Many of the people who come to me to take part in my 12-week Ignite Your Creativity course will also follow the similar journey of creating their businesses on their kitchen table. This has been a similar success story for many entrepreneurs throughout history who start their businesses from back rooms, bedrooms or kitchen tables. Steve Jobs and Steve Wozniak famously started Apple from home. They dropped out of their respective colleges to work on their business model and set up in Job's parents' garage in California. Michael Dell from Dell computers started his venture in college - from his dormitory as did Mark Zuckerberg with his Facebook idea while at Harvard. Sophia Amoruso, the founder of Nasty Gal clothing, started by selling pieces on eBay from her bedroom. One of my favourite rags to riches entrepreneurial stories is that of Jeff Bezos, who started Amazon as an online bookstore from his garage in

Washington in 1994.

You see, even the most prominent companies turning over millions (or billions in the case of Jeff Bezos and Amazon) were not in a position at first to invest in a separate office or warehouse or premises. I was the same with my candle making business. I started hand pouring my candles at my kitchen table before converting what used to be a downstairs bedroom in my home and then moving onto investing in my workshop space. Having a clear distinction between work and home time was important. With my young son at home with me, it couldn't be all work work work. I think this was helped by the energy of my house (as a home) from my love of Feng Shui and that's what I want to start by sharing.

The Energy in Your Home

Feng Shui has been around since 4000 BC and originates from China. There are some fundamental principles of Feng Shui to help the energy, flow and 'chi' within your home. Take these with a pinch of salt if this is not your thing, but they've helped me feel like my home flows well for the last three decades. When I come home from a long day teaching candle making or making bespoke label candles, I love the feeling of walking into my home immediately. I have set it up so that the principles of Feng Shui make it comforting, vibrant and full of life.

When starting to think about the Feng Shui in your home, think about the rooms that you don't tend to use as often. Are you avoiding certain spaces? Do they not feel great? What is it about those spaces that are not working?

In Feng Shui, the house is viewed as one whole being so each room must feel like it works and flows. Any room that does not work and flow would possibly benefit from a little Feng Shui energy.

Check Your Flow of Chi

The ancient Chinese believed that Feng Shui was the flow of energy or 'chi' in the home, and the front door is often regarded as the most crucial part. You can check your flow of chi in the home by closing your eyes and imagining water coming in with force through the front door. Are there any parts of the house that will never get wet? Are there things or clutter blocking the way? Does this chi get blocked before reaching your bedroom?

Sometimes all it takes is for an adjustment of furniture, placement of mirrors or a change in colour to uplift and energise the spaces in your home. Feng Shui is about feeling the power of connection between life and space.

Some Basic Feng Shui Tips for Your Home

Bathroom - Starting with the bathroom is the easiest Feng Shui adjustment. Always keep the door closed and the toilet seat down. Water goes out of the home here, and in Chinese tradition, water is a direct reflection of wealth. Keeping the toilet seat down is believed to help keep your money safe and not 'flushed away'. A true story from my friend, at one point in her life she needed a toilet seat that was raised as she couldn't lower herself down, the lid didn't lower down - what happened? She went into the red for the first time!

Front Door - Many homes use a driveway and back door as the entrance into the home. Feng Shui believes that the front door is the most important portal and gateway to the home's energy, so always use the front door to enter your home. Also, if your front door creaks or squeaks it is good Feng Shui practise to fix those audible niggles so that it doesn't affect your mood and annoy you as you walk into your home. Having a red door is very auspicious but since I'm a neutral lover I haven't quite brought myself to paint it red - maybe a red undercoat would work?

Bedroom - Position your bed centrally and out of the line of the bedroom door. This is known as the 'commanding' position. It is good practice to have two bedside tables on either side of the bed to balance the space. There should be plenty of room around the bed. Muted tones and candles or soft light help with the relaxing nature of the bedroom. You shouldn't place a mirror in your bedroom as that creates a 'third' person unless you can put a throw or pashmina over it when you are not using it. This applies to TV screens or computer monitors that might be in the room too. Also sleeping under beams can be harmful due to the sharp edges, but you can soften these with ivy or flowers.

Light - Light in your home is critical too, but direct harsh sunlight can have a negative effect. I don't have shutters on my office, so I hang a crystal in the window which catches the morning sunlight from the east and creates beautiful rainbows around the room which is also good for family harmony.

Fixing Things - It's good practice to attend to things that fall into disrepair as soon as you can. If light bulbs go out or things break in the home, I get quite passionate about sorting them out straight away. Like the time the gate was swinging off its hinges - it has to be sorted before it starts to add to low-level stress.

Clutter

Whether this is in your home or working space, clutter is not great for anyone. Even if you are the world's most free-thinking, spirited creative who thrives on the chaos of creation, the clutter will get to you eventually.

Creating the right environment in our homes and offices starts with getting rid of clutter. Physical clutter can cause mental clutter. For example, suppose you have sat at your desk and felt very unproductive but suddenly had a spurt of creativity or inspiration after you have cleaned your desk. In that case, that could be put down to the energy being cleared and getting ready to let new thoughts, ideas and motivation into your mindset.

Clutter that builds in the home often gets to a point where it becomes invisible. You end up walking over that same box in the hallway for months before doing something about it, or in the office, that same stack of books sits unread on your desk along with the paperwork that hasn't been touched and filed in weeks as the Fly Lady calls 'Hot spots'. Often we don't see this clutter as it becomes subconscious. A friend of mine calls this the "tolerables that become intolerable" and she uses a great example of the drawer of crap we all seem to have. Have you got one too? Either in your kitchen, bedroom or office? The drawer just seems to contain all the crap that has no home, and it builds and builds until one day as it threatens to vomit out the contents that you *really* see it. For the first time in a while, your eyes are opened. The thing that you have tolerated suddenly becomes intolerable.

The Home and Office Audit

You can stop the stress of getting to the position where the 'intolerables' drive you crazy by setting aside a time to do a home and office audit. Thinking of the Feng Shui principles of chi and energy flow, create a list of all the rooms in your home and your workspace.

As you move around your home, really look. Look so hard you cannot miss anything. Check all drawers and cupboards. Are things organised and easy to find? Are items put together? Does everything have a place and a definite home?

Are there things that are broken or no longer needed/useful? That drawer that always sticks, the picture that never seems to hang straight, the frayed carpet as you get into your bedroom. Make a list of all of these things, so you bring them into your awareness. It may take you several weeks to work from room to room to change these things or get organised, but the feeling of reduced physical and mental clutter afterwards is worth it.

If your clutter is a real problem, you could even try reading Marie Kondo's Life-Changing Magic of Tidying Up or watching her Netflix series Tidying Up with Marie Kondo. I have to be honest, I found her book quite extreme but if you need extreme in your life, if the clutter has got too much and you need inspiration, then her systematic method of tackling all the clutter in your home and workspace could help. I should say that I love her and dislike her in equal measures. In fact, I think her book is propping up my dining room table!

Your Work Environment

We touched on the clutter element of your working environment but where you work is also essential. If you are starting your business from home, try and have a specific working area.

You may not have the luxury of a home office, but you may be able to convert a room into a working space. If you have a spare bedroom that is currently used for guests, ask yourself how often people stay over? Could you convert this area into both an office and a guest space should you need the room for relatives? Many people struggle and make do with a home office space on the kitchen table when there's a whole room that could be dedicated to working. Did you buy your house to be a hotel for others or for it to work for you personally? Now that might not work if you're setting up a creative business as I did with candle making. I needed to be on the kitchen table (rather than taking candle wax upstairs into a spare room), but I also needed to find balance. I ended up converting what was a downstairs bedroom into a creative space where I could work on candle making and also have a space with the computer to do the admin side of the business.

The idea behind a dedicated space is to create a clear distinction between home time and work time. It is vital for your sanity and your family that you separate work from home life. This is to conserve and preserve your energy also. Having clear boundaries and time limits for work and home is a big help although I have to admit, I know this is something I could do more of. I love my business, and it enthuses me and leaves me energised, so I do find it hard to switch off. Having my workshop and that clear journey to and from work acts as a natural break between work and home, but I do still use my creative space that I converted from the front bedroom.

When writing this book in 2020, like the rest of the world, I was in lockdown due to the COVID-19 pandemic. I took my work home from my workshop for the duration and did find it difficult to have that distinction between home time and work time. Having no choice but to be home all the time was a great lesson in separating the spaces for work and home and mentally shutting off from the working day when every day felt the same and like Groundhog Day. There are small things you can do though like having a dedicated drawer or space where you clear your work things away at the end of the working day, or if you are lucky to have that home office space, agree a time you will finish work at home and shut the door on the office. Having that definite break and physical barrier to the computer and your work helps you shift from work mode into home and relaxation mode, which is so vital for every entrepreneur.

Your working area should always inspire you and leave you feeling great about your work. Trying to cram yourself into a small space or even working from your bed is often not conducive to feeling like you're in work mode. Remember I talked about 'dressing to the shoes' in the last chapter? That's a really good way to keep yourself in work mode in the home; otherwise, it is too tempting to lie in bed or lie on the sofa and feel like you're in relaxation mode.

However, there can be a time and a place for using more relaxing spaces and times for your work, and I do realise I sound a little like a hypocrite with what I am about to say. I'm not sure how it happened, but it seems that every few weeks, usually on a Tuesday I will get up at 5 am and take my laptop to the sofa, still in pyjamas and have what I call a 'Geek Day'. Now, I know this goes against all of the principles

I outlined in the last chapter and also everything I have just said about working from the sofa or bed, but this is a time I have come to love and cherish. I have found I am in the zone and in a state of flow so much that I don't have time to get dressed or move from the sofa. In fact, at the end of a 'Geek Day' session, my surroundings are usually pretty disgusting. I am still in my pyjamas, bowls and cups are all around me, and I may as well have formed myself into the sofa. But (big but coming), I plan these days in advance, and they are my pure indulgence with no expectation other than a day to immerse myself in learning or getting in the zone. These 'Geek Days' usually build up for me. I may have started a new programme or I've been reading a new book, and I'm excited to learn. The art of not getting dressed and not moving from the sofa comes from a place of excitement, wonder and giving myself permission to get so lost in research or geeking out that I am too engrossed to get dressed or move. I don't have any alerts on my devices, and on these days, when I am trying to get in 'flow', I don't use time management techniques like the Pomodoro technique where you work in 25 minute bursts and strict 5 minute breaks per half hour. I feel like this enforced way of working and sticking to time can interrupt my sense of being in 'flow'. I don't believe in multi-tasking, but when I'm geeking out, I like to have the tabs open with each project I have to work on that day. I always turn my email notifications off, so they don't wink at me when an email comes in.

In the same way, people might plan in self-care days involving a box set binge, I plan in a 'Geek Day' that is usually related to my work, but is always a definite form of self-care. The point here is that this is what works for me. Indulging in a day like this is my own personal appointment to shut off the rest of my work, and the rest of the world, while I chase my excitement.

When coming up with your own working environment, you will get to do the same. If you're planning on starting your own business while you work full time, you might find you also end up on the sofa in your PJs on the weekend while you learn all you can about your new venture. You might prefer to take yourself away to a cafe, coffee shop or co-working space to help you focus on your work. If you already run your own business, you might have a meeting room or a space or even a time that you allocate as 'protected time' where your team cannot disturb your work and flow. It is all about finding what working environment works for you personally. From the way you lay out your desk to the music or background noise you choose, the chair or space to choose to sit, or anything in between. The way we work and the way we work best is an entirely personal experience and one you will need to figure out what works best for you. We will cover more on the timings of work, particularly if you want to set up your own business in Chapter 5 - Your Ideal Day.

The Wider Ecological Environment

In addition to our own personal physical and mental environments and the environment in which we choose to work, there is also the wider ecology that is also very important to me.

Ever since I was a young girl in my small fishing village in Scotland, I have had a love, admiration and a lot of respect for the local environment. It has been part of who I am for as long as I can remember and I have an attitude of make do and mend, upcycling and demonstrating constant respect for our natural world. One of my heroes is David Attenborough. I was fascinated and enthralled by his Life On Earth book; I also had an atlas and would look with my mum at the places my dad would be travelling to in the Merchant Navy. I love rocks and geology; I would find fossils on the beach from a young age. I have a large plant lepidodendron fossil in my front garden, which they think could be 350,000,000 years old! I find fossils on the coastal path all the time, which is a constant source of wonder and delight.

I have actively chosen to demonstrate my love for all things to do with the environment, ecology and sustainability through my business. Sometimes this comes at a greater financial cost, but it is part of my core values to be the best guardian of the Earth that I can be, so it is important to me. I recycle and upcycle everything I can. I choose suppliers based on their own green manifestos and the way they conduct business and care for the environment. I never use single-use plastics and have made everything in my work sustainable - even down to no longer using pens in the workshop and instead using pencils made of recycled wood!

I believe that we all have a responsibility to protect our world for future generations, and business owners have a choice to be green and sustainable that goes deeper and far beyond just ticking boxes. When considering your own business and entrepreneurial path, I want to let you know that focusing on the immediate and wider environmental issues driven by climate change has benefitted me personally, my customers and my business. My customers are genuinely happy to see my commitment to being as environmentally friendly as possible. They understand why my prices might be that little percentage higher and appreciate the work that I do in the locality to help protect the environment for years to come. It has never harmed my business, choosing what I believe in over profits, and I think it is essential to share this with any would-be entrepreneur. It IS possible to have a profitable business when you aren't necessarily focusing on the profits, but you keep to your values, beliefs and the path you know you want to take on your business journey.

Chapter 5

Your Ideal Day

"Either you run the day or the day runs you."

-    Jim Rohn

I'm a big fan of motivational speaker and author, the late Jim Rohn. One of his teachings is that either you run the day or the day runs you. I firmly believe this and know it to be true. The moment I was able to reclaim my days and run them in a way that worked for me, my family and my business was the time in which my life and business changed.

If you are someone reading this book who wants to establish their own business, you have to plan your days in advance and get clear on what you're capable of achieving in a full day. It's probably more than you realise and with a few small tweaks, you will be amazed at how much you can pack into your day and move the needle on your goals quicker than you have ever done before.

Before I discovered the power of a morning routine, my mornings were spent hunched wearily over a cup of coffee - waiting for the caffeine hit to take hold and shake my body out of its slumber. I'd probably turn the news on and find out what was happening in the world. Even on my long haul flying days, this was the routine. There was something comforting and familiar as the jingle for BBC World Service would play. It would always connect me to home, but the problem with watching this on waking was it did not set me up for the day. BBC World Service takes the news from all over the world. As we know, the media is always more geared up to share the negative, sensational and shocking news from around the world. Filling my mind with the horrors of war, natural disasters and the world's most shocking crimes was not a great and positive way to start my day. It would put my mindset in a state of panic as the media hype would affect my emotions.

I have never struggled to get out of bed in the morning. I've always been disciplined at getting up, which started in childhood. My mum wasn't a single mum, but as my dad was away with the Merchant Navy for months on end, my mum could be a bit of a tyrant, and there's one thing she would never let me do, and that was sleeping in. I was never allowed to lay in bed, even if I were ill, I wouldn't be allowed to lay in bed until lunchtime. Mum had a coffee shop and an antique business, and we were always up and out, busy and productive from an early hour. That work ethic has stayed with me until adulthood. Even now, I am not someone who can lie in or just slob on the sofa all day. My parents would never let me do that, and so that is part of who I am as a person.

That being said, even though my whole life had been productive mornings, I did not realise just what I was capable of until I discovered a book that would change my life. It was on a trip to

Harry Potter Studios down south that I discovered a book that would have such a positive impact. We stopped at Abingdon service station for petrol and refuelling. I love to have a nosey in the book shops, and I saw a book that caught my eye. It was Hal Elrod's The Miracle Morning which stood out. I remember thinking "Mornings? A miracle? What is miraculous about mornings?" and I bought the book. I read that book on my journey to and from Harry Potter Studios and started to put a morning routine into practice as soon as I got home.

I encourage you to read Hal Elrod's book, whether you have a morning routine or not, you will get something from it. Without giving too much of the book away, I started to do things I had never done before, like get up at 5 am out of choice and meditate. Up until this point, I was only waking up around 7:30-8 am and doing the school run then getting on with my day. When I realised I could swap my day around and get to bed earlier to get up earlier, I could achieve more.

The Life-Changing Magic of Meditation

Hal Elrod's book gets you to follow a specific structure for your morning routine. It was the first time my mornings had ever had a structure, and it made a positive impact from day one. I was amazed at what I could achieve in a short space of time and how accomplished I could feel. I was also speaking to myself in a new positive way and trying out new skills that had not been on my radar before. I had never tried to meditate in the past and found myself looking for guided meditations on YouTube.

While the meditations were good, I didn't know what I was doing. It was at the forefront of my mind when I noticed a poster jump out at me at the local Town Hall. It was for meditation classes with a lady called Adele. I phoned her to ask about the classes and instantly felt drawn and connected to this wonderful and wise lady with the voice of an angel who was about to teach me how to connect to myself using meditation.

At the first class, there were only three of us (I now know I was the first person to respond to Adele's poster for the class). It was so powerful that it was too much. She is an inspirational mature lady with the most beautiful wrinkle-free skin. She is such a sense of comfort in my life, and I adore our conversations. In those early meditation classes, she ignited something within me, and my meditations were so deep I was scared. I felt like there was nothing before me, behind me or around me. It was like I was suspended in space and scared me a little. I ended up having a panic attack when I came round from my meditation. It did not deter me as I could see how positive the meditations were. They allowed me to slow down, which is precisely what I needed at the time.

As my love of meditation continued, I found new resources to continue my practise as part of my Miracle Morning routine. I started to meditate to YouTube videos that focused on the teachings of Dr Wayne Dyer and his 'I am' meditation. He practices meditation using the Moses Code frequency meditations which are created using tuning forks. He uses the ancient Kabbalah system of assigning specific numbers to words finding the sounds that correspond to 'I am that I am' the words that God spoke when Moses asked for God's name in the book of Exodus in the Old Testament. If you search for 'I am that I am' meditation on YouTube, you will find these meditations. Many people feel that these meditations bring them closer to God. I am not religious, but I do find these meditations powerful.

Another guided meditation type is following the Solfeggio scales or Solfeggio frequencies. These are six tones that are set to bring the body back into alignment and healing. The Solfeggio frequencies were believed to have come from the ancient world and were used in Indian Sanskrit teachings alongside the chants of Gregorian Monks. In the 1970s, Dr Joseph Puleo rediscovered the frequencies and brought their benefits back into public awareness. In 1988, biochemist Dr Glen Rein tested how the different frequencies impacted human DNA. The Georgian and Sanskrit chants had a positive and healing effect on human DNA.

My Solfeggio meditation takes me through all the different frequencies in a body scan exercise, that I find sets me up for the day, but also allows me to tune into my own body and how I am really feeling. It gives me that moment and opportunity in the morning to check in with both my mental and physical health and well-being. A couple of years later, I invested in some singing bowls to enhance this audio experience in meditation. They are set to certain hertz, and when I run the wand around the bowl, the tone not only brings about a feeling of calm, but I feel it physically too in my body. I often sit and think how on earth I lived my life without meditation. It is one of the true joys and pleasure I have in my life, and the positive effects it has on my brain cannot be ignored. I will also sometimes use meditation as a moment to ask for things that I have lost. I have sat and meditated many times on things I have misplaced, and the answer has appeared in meditation.

Following The Miracle Morning structure, I was also able to repeat affirmations to myself every morning. Affirmations are positive statements you can repeat to yourself verbally or write them down to reaffirm a belief. Saying affirmations feels very strange at first - especially if you have never done anything like this before. Many of us are guilty of speaking to ourselves in such harsh and negative terms, but this practice made me feel instantly uplifted. When I first picked up The Miracle Morning, Hal Elrod offered a lot of digital downloads to assist your journey in establishing a morning routine. I printed off a list of affirmations to get me used to this practice and would tick them off daily as I said them to myself. It gave me something to follow and a structure. I would repeat things like "I am strong" and then when I would head out on my morning runs, I found myself repeating some of these statements with every step. I swear it would make me run faster, easier and lighter on my feet. This was all new to me, but I saw the benefits immediately. I swear reading The Miracle Morning opened up a whole new world for me.

Visualise Your Day Ahead

Visualisation became a part of my morning routine on reading The Miracle Morning, but I realised I had always done this in some shape or form. As an artist, I am a visual person, and I have always visualised things in my life. Being able to see something through gives you the discipline needed at times to progress with action steps on a project. If you can clearly see the end goal in your mind, you are more determined to get there.

I had used visualisation daily for many years. When flying long haul, I would visualise what I was wearing, my journey to work, the passengers I would meet, and the tasks I would have that day. I would run the day in my mind like a movie reel before it had even happened. This would ensure I packed the right things and left on time. I love to be on time, I hate being late, so running through the day in my mind in advance meant I was always prepared. I do this thing called 'the day before the day before' so if something has to be done say, on a Friday I will have it ready for the Thursday. I apply it to most things in my life. Nothing is left until the actual day. I even visualise getting these things done early.

This is one of the best ways to use visualisation - especially if you are an entrepreneur. Using visualisation to clearly see your dream business in the future will keep you motivated to take action to get you there. But using visualisation at a very basic daily level will also mean that your day should hopefully go OK with a bit of forward planning.

You can visualise your day ahead the night before. Check your diary and your emails/messages. Who needs you? When and where? Visualise what you have coming up the following day and ask yourself these questions;

- What do you have coming up in your diary tomorrow?
- What will you need for the day ahead to make it a success?
- What could you prepare right now that might reduce the stress and decision fatigue tomorrow morning?
- What can you get ready and set out now to help you tomorrow?
- What time will you need to leave?
- Who do you need to connect with tomorrow and what is the best way to do that?

Try and run how you think the whole day will go like a movie on fast forward and feel prepared before you head to bed.

Many people do not realise that they can choose how their day goes, and a combination of affirmations and visualisation make this process a lot easier. Have you ever had a morning where you jump out of bed, stub your toe and then that's it you declare the day to be awful before it has even started. What happens? The day is usually awful because you have chosen it to be. That is your mood, and nothing is going to shake it. Many people don't realise that they can choose how they feel through positive affirmations or visualising how a day will go with positivity rather than negativity or fear. The way we talk to each other and the way we talk to ourselves, even in our heads is so vitally important. That includes a visualisation of the day ahead. Let's say you're going to have to deal with someone who is unpleasant or have a difficult conversation, why not plough your energy into making the visualisation of that chat positive? If you go into a discussion with confrontational, negative energy that is probably the way the chat will go. Suppose you visualise it to be something positive, open, transparent and a good learning exercise. In that case, you will use language to match that, and hopefully the meeting and interaction will go more smoothly. Visualise the outcome that you want and your energy will match in that situation. This includes the way you talk to yourself and about yourself in your own mind. This is the most important part of a morning routine. If you talk to yourself in such a bad way and start your day with negative self-talk, then I believe you are inviting other people to talk to you like that too. It is so important the way we speak to ourselves.

Eat That Frog

It was Brian Tracy who wrote the book 'Eat That Frog' which is all about the power of doing the jobs you hate first. The premise is that if you had a list of things to do but 'eat a frog' was on the list if you eat the frog first and get it out of the way all of the other tasks will feel easier to achieve. If you put off the frog all day, you will have that in your mind, and it will make you less productive on your other tasks.

I always try and adopt this principle and do the worst job first. There is always something in your diary that you go *"Urgh, I can't believe I have to do that!"* or a task that is your least favourite thing to do. For me, it would be something like inputting important business data into a spreadsheet. As much as I dislike this job, I would always try and do it as the first task of the day outside of my Miracle Morning steps, so it is done, off my list and out of my consciousness. This is also otherwise known as delayed gratification - doing the things you don't want to do before the things you enjoy doing. It is a powerful life skill, and it is something that I try to teach my son.

Exercise

My ideal day always has some form of exercise. There is something about getting your blood pumping and your heart racing that makes you feel alive. When I first discovered The Miracle Morning, I realised one of the steps was to exercise. I was delighted. I was training to run a marathon at the time, and suddenly the training did not seem as daunting. Getting up at 5 am and running was so enjoyable. There was a small group of us dedicated 5 am running crazy people who would get out and do a quick hour of running a few mornings a week. We called ourselves 'the sunrise group' because we would loop around the village but always end up running on the coastal path. Depending on the time of year, we would often have the absolute pleasure of seeing the sunrise over the sea and illuminate our little fishing village. It was always the most breathtaking sunrise. Even if the weather was not that great, there was something magical about the sun breaking through the horizon. It would always be golden and glowing before the clouds would set in, and the rain would fall. If we were lucky, we might even get to see dolphins swim by.

I often felt sorry for all the people slumbered in their beds who would not get the chance to see the majestic sight of the sunrise as we did. It was the jewel of the day. On the way back from sun gazing we would call in at the village bakers and take a bit of money with us to buy hot rolls or bread for breakfast. It was idyllic and always the best start to the day in any weather. It made me feel alive. I would not hit snooze and never be tempted to stay in bed because my fellow running nutters would be standing waiting for me in the park raring to go. If you could say no once, you could say no twice, so I was strict in always showing up. I would put my running gear out the night before, so I could fall out of bed, get dressed and get into my running shoes. You just felt like you were set up for the day. I have heard some runners even go as far as to sleep in their running gear!

In 2020 I tried a 30-day yoga challenge with a lovely lady on YouTube called Adriene - you may have come across her videos? I have been doing this for three months now, and I cannot believe how much I have progressed, I can do a handstand for a whole minute - something I always thought would be impossible for someone like me. I am just so glad I have found something that I can still do in the morning that sets my mind and body up for the day. I miss the sunrise running sessions, but the structure and flexibility of yoga has filled that void.

Wim Hof Breathing Method

This is a relatively new thing for me, but I already can feel the benefits. I have added Wim Hof breathing techniques into my morning routine after finding a three-day challenge he hosts online. If you haven't heard of him, Wim Hof otherwise known as 'The Iceman' is a Dutch extreme athlete known for enduring cold temperatures for long periods of time. He is famous for climbing Mount Everest in his underpants and doing the Antarctic marathon barefoot. Hof has been the subject of several medical assessments and a book by investigative journalist Scott Carney. He is a comical man from the Netherlands, and I love listening to him speak and watching his videos. He always makes me giggle with his words "hooly in" meaning "fully in!" Amongst the good-natured humour is a man that is so dedicated to his craft. Many famous people have adopted the Wim Hof methods including Tim Ferris and Lewis Howes who talk about this regularly on their podcasts, and both have great episodes with Wim Hof that can be enjoyed at your leisure to learn more about him. Hof's wife died by suicide, leaving him to care for four young children who were going through the most extreme grief and pain. Feeling like life had lost all meaning, he came across a freezing cold stream in the Netherlands where he lives. Not really understanding why he wanted to, he got into the stream and noticed the impact the cold had on his body, particularly with his breathing. He was drawn back to the cold water and started this practice each morning. Over the years this led him to develop the Wim Hof Method (WHM) which involves three "pillars": cold therapy, breathing and meditation. It has similarities to Tibetan Tummo meditation and pranayama, both of which employ breathing techniques.

I had heard about him because one of the practitioners that works for my husband in his rehabilitation clinic is trained in the method. They put an event on about the Wim Hof Method because this practitioner could now hold his breath for six minutes after following the Wim Hof Method. At the time, I didn't think it was something I would be interested in. How wrong I was!

I first came across him after getting his book Becoming the Iceman. I read his book, and while a lot of it I could discard, I was super fascinated by the effect his methods have on illnesses like diabetes, MS, autoimmune conditions, asthma and common diseases. I was fascinated because I have asthma, so I was tuned into this. I found his website and three-day mini-course. I loved it, and after I followed his techniques, I instantly felt a connection with my body. I then downloaded his app and got into the cold water immersion alongside the breathing techniques.

Before adopting the Wim Hof Method, I could probably hold my breath for 10 or 20 seconds. I did his first lot of breathing and held my breath for a minute "oh that was weird" I thought to myself and thought there must be something to this. He is a really funny character, and I love how he has all these World records but dismisses them as "Stupid records" and says he does what he does because of the positive effect of health on the body. The next stage of his technique is cold water therapy. My shower wasn't cold enough to do this, so I got my son to hook up the hose pipe outside for me to go under it in my swimming costume. I know this sounds extreme and a little like madness. It is a gradual process getting into the cold. I do my hands first, then my feet before putting my body under the cold hose. I feel so amazing and invigorated, and I would go as far to say I almost feel a bit high. I now have my daily shower outside, and I can honestly say it's the best shower I have ever had, standing in the sunrise with the birds tweeting. It isn't something I'm advising you to do for your own ideal day; it is once again a reminder that getting out of your comfort zone can be deeply powerful. You could even try switching the shower to cold at the end of your daily shower to give you a mini taste of how this can invigorate you and set you up for the day. To take this practice one step further, I have ordered a giant whisky barrel which has just arrived (much to the amusement of my husband and son!). I am planning on filling it with cold water and ice and seeing how long I can withstand it. The funny thing is it still has some malt whisky in the bottom, and the aroma is so powerful. I'm going to come out smelling like a distillery!

Bolt Things Together to Maximise Your Time

I have always been a big fan of bolting tasks together to make the most out of your time. For example, while the kettle is boiling, I'm usually found doing press-ups against the worktop! Or when I'm doing my morning beauty regime, I am often listening to an audiobook at the same time.

While I am working, I like to listen to audiobooks or interesting perspectives from talks on the Gaia app and website. I find that I can't listen to music much anymore because I would prefer to bolt tasks together and I love to learn so much. When I'm pouring candles, I listen to language apps when I don't have to concentrate. I am learning Mandarin and Spanish at the moment but previously had been learning Japanese. Whether I am actively listening or not, I find that it does go in subconsciously. I can be listening while I am putting hundreds of wicks in candles and think I am not paying attention but the next day when I come back to the language app, what I have listened to comes back into my head. I like to call this food for the brain. In Dr Chatterjee's Book, Feel Better in 5, he talks about having 'mind snacks' five times a day which means feeding your brain with things that are positive and good for brain function.

You will always find me listening and learning something when I'm doing household chores, on a walk or a run or working. I know we all have the same amount of hours and minutes in a day, but you will be amazed at what you can get done when you bolt it onto other things. I also like to learn when I am in the car. I rarely listen to music or the radio; I will hook my phone up to the car stereo and find something on YouTube or Audible before we set off. Something like a speech from Jim Rohn or Bob Proctor. I love listening to these people as they are or were, experts in their field and there is a lot to learn from them. The drive to school is 15 minutes each day which gives me 1 hour and 15 minutes of active listening time on that one journey each week. I don't want to waste it; I will always bolt my learning onto the car journeys.

This is a Gift

Getting up at 5 am is a definite discipline. Sometimes when I wake up naturally, I hear this voice say "This is a gift". I hear it, and I answer back "I know, but I'm just going to lie here for 10 minutes" but that voice saying it is a gift keeps going round and round in my head. I think of all the things I could be doing, I am reminded how much I love these early mornings to myself to set me up for the day, and I get out of bed with a small spring in my step.

Many books on business will tell you about a morning routine and getting up early. For most people, this could sound like pure torture. That is why reframing it as a gift is so important. You will be amazed at what you can achieve when you give yourself space and time to have a great and structured morning routine. You feel ahead of the game with all you have achieved, and you are ready for the day. Your mindset is strong, you feel motivated to tackle your tasks, and you can achieve your goals quicker.

If you are going to adopt a morning routine, it is equally as important to adopt an evening routine where you power down effectively ready for bed to get the rest you need to do it all over again the next day.

As a rule, I don't answer work emails after dinner or on a Sunday and dinner time is a very important moment for us as a family. We will sit and eat at the dinner table without any screens, and I make a point of us doing this. It is too easy for each of us in the family to get lost in our own projects and so coming together to connect over our evening meal is non-negotiable.

I don't watch much TV either, and if it's not a documentary or something I have been consuming on Gaia the alternative TV channel and app, then I will generally head to bed just after 9 pm. I will visualise the next day and get things ready that I may need, but I will be in bed with a book just after 9 pm and asleep by 10 pm. This is a routine and timings that have worked for me so well in the last few years, and if you're someone who is trying to run their own business but have time for themselves and personal goals, then I would highly recommend this way.

My 5-9, 9-5, 5-9 Method ™

In 2019 I created my first online 12-week course and membership programme called Ignite Your Creativity. I worked hard on this course, as it was something I was desperate to create and launch. I have had many business owners come to my workshops and ask for advice on setting up their own business, so I wanted to distil my knowledge and expertise in a format that would be easy to follow, hold people accountable and see people achieve side hustles that turn into full-time businesses in a short space of time.

When working on this course, I adopted the 5-9, 9-5, 5-9 Method ™ to ensure I could create it while running my business. I knew I needed to carve out additional time in my day so I decided I would shorten my Miracle Morning practice to an hour between 5-6 am, then use 6-9 am as my time to work on this project. The next time block, 9-5 pm, was my time to be in my actual business pouring candles and hosting workshops as usual. Once home after collecting my son from school, the 5-9 pm block was reserved for family dinner and then working on the course. I did this from February to October from Monday morning to Friday at 5 pm, leaving the weekends reserved for family time. It allowed me the brain space and the time I knew I needed to put into developing the course. I am so proud of my achievements and the discipline I displayed at this time. It paid off without compromising my energy levels. My work always enthuses me, so it was a treat and a joy to work on something I was so passionate about. The course was launched and continues to be successful in teaching other would-be business owners how to juggle their family commitments, personal goals and careers with the business they know they have brewing. If you are serious about your future dreams and your business, then sometimes you have to make sacrifices. There is a great quote which states 'If you do what you love then you will never work a day in your life'. I help people realise this and make their business dreams come to fruition. Yes, it might be a little bit tiring at first, but there is a real joy and a sense of achievement in putting the time aside for your future dreams, goals and earning potential. You will get more out of life in the future if you dedicate that time to your business right now. There is magic, and there is money to be made when you dedicate time to your future rather than using your free time to binge on a box set or mindless scrolling on social media. Put in the work, and you will surely reap the rewards.

Get Your Rocks in First

Have you seen the time management exercise involving rocks, pebbles, sand and a glass jar? This is a visual representation exercise designed to make you prioritise the most important things in life.

You complete this exercise twice. The first time you take the sand first, place it in the jar and then follow up with pebbles and finally try to fit the rocks in. It doesn't work! Yet if you repeat the exercise by placing the rocks in first, then the pebbles and finally carefully pour the sand in, it trickles in the gaps, and you fit everything into the jar.

The sand represents all the unimportant things in your life. The rocks represent the major and most important things in life, then the pebbles with medium importance and then the sand represents the things in life with low importance. You might have also heard this story with golf balls and sand - sometimes that visual is used. The point is that you must prioritise the rocks or golf balls first. Get those in your jar of life first and make everything else fit around it. I talk more about how this works for me personally in Chapter 9 - Mastering the Work/Life Challenge.

Exercise: Your Ideal Day - What Does it Look Like?

Start with your important 'Rocks': family, health, job and appointments. What absolutely must get done in your ideal day?

Next, think about the pebbles - the stuff that is still important and has to be done, but if it isn't done, it isn't a tragedy. Think about things like household chores.

Finally, the sand is about unimportant tasks that are not urgent. For you, this might be wasting time on social media.

When thinking about this exercise, it is also really important to schedule in time to do nothing - this is space for something new to come in. If there is no space then nothing new will arrive, just think of it like a glass of water, if it is full you can't welcome anything else. Same as a diary.

Rocks -
    1.
    2.
    3.

Pebbles -
    1.
    2.
    3.

Sand -
    1.
    2.
    3.

In the workbook that accompanies this book, there is an exercise for you to map out your current daily routine and start to think about what your ideal day would look like. If you haven't downloaded your workbook yet, please visit jomacfarlane.com/bonus to get yours direct to your inbox.

Chapter 6

Ask & Act

"You get in life what you have the courage to ask for."

- Oprah Winfrey

How many times have you heard that phrase throughout your lifetime? It's something that is taught to us from an early age and is especially ingrained in those of us who run our own businesses. While it can sometimes feel daunting and embarrassing to ask for what we want, it is a vital skill. In Scotland, we have a phrase 'A gawin fit aye gets' (translated to "A going foot always gets") which conjured up images of people who are proactive and things happen for them. The phrase means if you are prepared, you will be presented with opportunity. If you are ready for something, you'll receive it.

For me, one of the most powerful ways to ask for what you want is to use manifesting to ask for what you desire out of your life or work. Manifesting works by asking and visualising what you desire and being grateful for it before it happens. Manifesting is when you believe something to have happened before the event has occurred. People manifest in different ways, but many will decide what they want to have, be or do and then visualise it as if it has already happened.

I am not sure when my relationship and love affair with manifesting started. As a small child, I adopted beachcombing. I would trawl the pebbled beaches near my home with my mother and seek out washed out items that could be transformed and loved. My childhood was like a permanent treasure hunt, and I'd often set out on my sandy adventures with a heart full of hope to find something sparkly or exciting. I would regularly seek out lost jewellery, discarded money or beautiful pearlescent shells on the sandy shores. I would find marbles, tiny porcelain dolls and fill my old printer's tray full of small treasures - usually after wishing and hoping and praying that something would turn up on my scavenger hunts. I made a connection early on that if I asked for it, what I desired would often turn up.

Years later, in my adulthood, I have become an avid devotee of manifesting. I believe if you ask for what you want that The Universe delivers. I know this is a hard concept for some people to fathom. I was once at a business event, sharing a space with a woman who was an artist and an academic. We got onto the topic of manifesting, and she looked at me with a furrowed brow as if I was completely insane. I could see she wasn't getting it and so the conversation went something like this;

"To test it out, pick something small at random. Ask for it, and over the next week, see if that thing comes into your life. Go on, pick something specific to look out for."

"A yellow butterfly". She replied, obviously humouring me because the chances of this appearing in a Scottish seaside village were slim to none. Alas, there is always hope. I told her to believe it would appear and had a little moment myself where I visualised a yellow butterfly.

Later in the day, the owner of the venue where we were displaying our crafts popped in with afternoon tea for us. She handed the cups of tea out, and on the mug, she handed to my academic artist companion was none other than a yellow butterfly! She was shocked, still very sceptical but agreed to look into it more.

I have so many stories of asking for certain items and them turning up on my lap or doorstep. It has got to the point now, where I laugh about the weird and wonderful ways my wishes are delivered to me. I have also got my young son Archie involved in my requests to The Universe. If you indulge me a moment, I'll tell you some amazing manifestation stories and encourage you to participate yourself, making it like a game.

Raising your Vibration

Everything on the planet has a vibration. From the table to the wall, potato in the kitchen to the grass. It was Einstein who said, "Everything in life is vibration."

Have you ever found yourself saying "They were not my vibe at all" where someone you have met might not have clicked with you? Scientists will tell you this is when two types of energy don't gel. You might say about someone "They're on my wavelength!" meaning they're on the same vibration as you.

Sir David Hawkins was a renowned psychiatrist and spiritual teacher who aimed to bring scientific meaning into spiritual practices. He created the Scale of Consciousness to display different emotions we experience as a sliding scale. In Hawkins' map, different states of consciousness are mapped on a scale of 1–1000. With 1000 representing figures like the Buddha and 20 being the lowest levels of shame and guilt.

According to the scale, if you are on a low vibration, you will attract more of the same.

Here is how the scale works:

Enlightenment	700 - 1000
Peace	600
Joy	540
Love	500
Reason	400
Acceptance	350
Willingness	310
Neutrality	250
Courage	200
Pride	175
Anger	150
Desire	125
Fear	100
Grief	75
Apathy	50
Guilt	30
Shame	20

Have you ever had a morning where nothing seems to go right? You rush around, get caught in the rain or miss your train? Before you know it, you are saying "it's going to be one of these days" and guess what? You are right! Your day continues to go from bad to worse with a series of misfortunes because you are in a state of anger and frustration. What you think and believe the mind will achieve. Like attracts like so if you are always in a negative state, negative things will happen to you.

On the scale of consciousness, anger resides around the 150 mark on the scale. Shame sits at the lowest end with a score of 20. At the other end is enlightenment, vibrating at 700-1000. We are born neutral at 250, and the good news is we can choose to raise our vibe, to higher levels. Hawkins stated we could do this by choosing positive self-talk, affirmations, eating good food like fresh vegetables, not animals that have been killed through pain and suffering, avoiding alcohol and coffee. That's why people who perform therapies like Reiki are encouraged to adopt a vegetarian lifestyle. Those who are Buddhists also adopt a lifestyle free from meat, fish and stimulants like caffeine and alcohol.

Love and gratitude raise your vibe and listening to positive vibe music like classical music raises your vibration. Music, like heavy metal with negative lyrics, changes the vibration. According to Hawkins, the vibe at which heavy metal music transmits to our ears is potentially bad for our heart health. According to a study by gigwise.com participants' hearts narrowed by 6% when listening to stressful music. Can you think of a piece of music that makes you feel good? And one that makes you feel bad? You will no doubt resonate and vibrate at a similar level to the song that you love and repel against the vibe or wavelength of the song you dislike.

"As you think, you vibrate. As you vibrate, you attract." –Abraham-Hicks

In Abraham Hicks' work on moving up the scale on the law of attraction, it isn't the scale of consciousness that is used but an emotional guidance scale. This scale is in two parts and ranges across 22 different emotions. Eleven of which point upwards and raise your emotional guidance and eleven point downwards and decrease your level awareness with your inner being.

The teachings of Abraham Hicks suggests that in order to benefit from the law of attraction and attract your desires into your life, you must work on cultivating the right emotions that will help push you upwards on the trajectory to achieving your desires. Joy, knowledge, love and appreciation sit at the top level of this spiral. So when you have the knowledge of what you want, you can practice gratitude and appreciation for it (before it has even happened) you will experience the joy of bringing it to fruition.

Learning where you are on the scale at any one time, with different areas of your life will help you measure whether you need to focus on driving your vibration upwards or not. For more information on this Google 'The Emotional Guidance Scale'.

When you are vibrating at the wrong level, you won't get what you ask for. I have a funny story that demonstrates this well.

The Million Pounds that Turned Up On my Doorstep

I was having a particularly challenging day in the candle business that I run. I am usually unflappable, positive, and I can always find a way out of a challenge or a problem, but on this particular day, I felt like the world was conspiring against me. What I did next is not normally part of my daily routine, I was stressed and getting anxious and in a moment of desperation looked upwards as if I were asking the angels directly and shouted at the top of my voice "Please PLEASE if it is within your power, PLEASE can you give me £1 million? This would solve all my daily problems!"

I immediately felt a little better at having released my frustration and set about trying to work myself out of my challenging day. I kid you not, a mere 15 minutes later my doorbell rang. I was still in my semi, angry rage and was straining to put a smile on my face for whoever was at the door. It was a friend returning some of the guide books that I had loaned her for a recent trip to New York. Also, to say thank you for the loan of the books, she handed me a gift from her travels.

The gift was a bar of chocolate in the shape and style of a £1m dollar note and not only that the company that made the chocolate was Bartons (Barton is my married name). I didn't share with her what had happened in the previous 15 minutes as I'm sure she would have thought I was complete bonkers. But I laughed so hard after she left, I thought that's what I deserve, I didn't ask specifically for monetary £1m, so they delivered what they saw fit. So be very specific what you ask for!

Getting Specific on Asking for What You Desire

Asking for what you desire isn't just about manifesting the dream house or the dream car, it is about asking for help, guidance and ways to be.

In the accompanying online workbook to this book, I encourage you to sit down and truly focus on what you want to be, do and have. At the end of this chapter, I have added a short section to focus on the three most important things, but in the workbook, we go into much more depth. I encourage you to sit awhile and really feel into what you want to be, do and have and keep that list in your workbook. I have done this myself with 100 things in each category. It was quite difficult at first to fill each column in. I felt silly asking for things that seemed wildly ambitious and played down my desires. Then I thought about it from a child's perspective. If I were a child, I would dream big. The world would be my oyster, and I would not hold back. So complete the 100 list with full gusto and fill in your wildest dreams and desires along with the smaller stuff. Keep that list to hand, revisit it often and put a little heart by the ones you achieve. You will be surprised what comes to fruition!

What is important to mention is that it doesn't matter HOW you are going to do, be or get something; all you need to know is that you DESIRE it. The Universe works in the most amazingly mysterious ways to conspire to make things happen for you, you just believe. This is so important to me and very much a part of who I am. You will often find me holding my hands out, even if driving, I will often stop, pull over and open my palms up. "I am open, I am open, I am open," I say three times to signify that I am open to receiving what is right for me at that moment in time. You have to be open to anything and just because you have one thing doesn't mean you can't have another. Your motorhome doesn't have to compromise your holiday to Spain - you could have both. Also don't think that you either don't deserve everything you desire and don't feel like you can't ask for what you want in case it is taken from someone else. Don't think about how just think about your desire. Always be open to any help, love and abundance. It sounds all a bit Disney, but trust me, try it for yourself and see what can be brought into reality for you.

Visualising becoming a Triathlete

When I started training for my first triathlon, I really focused on visualising it becoming a reality for me. Blending the three disciplines of swimming, cycling and then running was new to me, and I was anxious and worried about being good enough. I cut out a picture of a triathlon medal and popped it in my vision box where I keep other visual tools or pictures of things that I would like to bring into reality. I visualised that at the end of the triathlon, I would take a picture of my real triathlon medal when I held it in my hands alongside the one I'd cut out. I think it was over a year that little picture sat in the box, I would take it out every now and then and hold it in my hands and think and feel what it would be like to be a triathlete. I spent a lot of time watching YouTube videos on 'transitioning' from one discipline to another and also visualising myself doing it. Studies have shown it is more powerful if you can see yourself in the first person (where you can see around yourself) than in the third person when you are looking at yourself. Watching someone else do the action or task stimulates the same area of the brain (putamen) if you were to do it yourself. Science shows that athletes who do visualisation, alongside physical practice, show improved results over those who have just practised according to a study conducted by Feltz and Landers in 1983.

The day it came to fruition was a magnificent day for me, not for anyone else because I believe you are your own cheerleader. If you are waiting for someone to stand by your bed in the morning encouraging you that you need to get out and run or jump in the pool at silly o'clock, that you need to exercise for your own health, and if you're waiting for someone to stand by the swimming pool counting your lengths for you, good luck! The day I completed my triathlon felt surreal. I am not a triathlete at all but crossing the bridge into something new and taking on the challenge really helped me believe in myself even more. I celebrated with euphoria at reaching this goal and I also celebrated that I didn't come last too!

It would've been really easy for me to focus on not being fast enough or having the best gear. Those things would possibly put you off even entering in the first place! I think it is more important to just show up rather than get stressed and obsessed with the best times. I believe that showing up and getting stuff done triumphs all obsession with perfection. You need to get the hell out of your own way and get shit done. People blame all sorts of things, their time, other influences, even other people. Imagine blaming your husband or significant other for your own fitness or diet, don't put your key to health and fitness in someone else's pocket! Do it for your mind, body and soul. Make yourself accountable.

'You can't hire someone to do your push-ups for you' – Jim Rohn.

What you don't know is that I couldn't even swim when I cut the triathlon medal out. In that event, I was actually last out of the swimming pool, and the other entrants clapped me! I made up the time with my cycle and run though and at least wasn't last.

I knew that swimming was not my strongest point. Being brought up on the beach in a tiny fishing village, my family home was 20ft from the beach. I could 'float' but not swim. I have enormous respect and fear for the sea; it has huge power. I remember standing as a child one stormy night, breathless and terrified, the word passed around the village that a fishing boat had gone down the wrong channel towards the safety of the harbour and was stuck unable to move. The helicopter was trying to winch the fishermen off one by one which was a painstakingly slow process while you watched the men on the deck, only a few feet from the shore but completely helpless with the boat breaking up underneath their wellies. A lot of the older fishermen don't swim, and they don't wear lifejackets either. I believe there is a campaign now to insist they wear them.

Before embarking on my triathlon, I knew I needed help. My son was being taught to swim at the time, and I messaged his swim teacher to see if she'd take me on as a client. I literally could swim no more than three 'no style' strokes (badly and gulping in vast amounts of water at the same time). Laurie, my friend and swim coach, was so patient, but I could see her face and sense the challenge ahead. I followed her advice and managed the triathlon. I joined a triathlon club and was utterly terrified the first night I went along. I was shattered after just the warm-up, but what was important was hanging out with people who ate, slept and trained in all things triathlon. I'd ask so many questions from what to wear, when and what to eat, how to swim, how to transition and asked for advice on the best gear to purchase to help my efforts. I was well and truly out of my comfort zone. I'd study past results of races to see if I could complete it before the last person had crossed the line. I went from doing a Super Sprint to Sprint and then registered for a Middle Distance Ironman where there was a cut off time of 8.5 hours. I knew I could finish it, but the time would be tight. It was such a good feeling achieving what I had visualised for such a long time. I didn't want to leave it there so decided to partake in more swim challenges to really push my limits.

I swam the English Channel (virtually in a pool) all 22 miles of it in 2018 and did the challenge this time in open water in 2019. I wondered how I'd manage in the three autumnal months September through December, already encountering jellyfish and standing on a fish. I had hoped to achieve it before November. Tide timetable purchased and all the dates highlighted that the tide would be 'swimmable' that isn't taking into account weather and other factors. It was hard enough trying to complete this in a pool, but I thought I couldn't do the same swim again could I, that wouldn't be a challenge.

Taking on sporting challenges is a mix of asking and acting for me. There is only a certain amount of visualising of the end result success that you can do. Not taking action won't get you over that finish line in the way you envisaged. But visualising success helps inspire you into action. This is where I think the Universe can conspire to pull people towards you and help make it happen in the way you are hoping, wishing and dreaming.

So if you want it badly enough, you can do it. "How do you eat an Elephant? – One bite at a time" this phrase always makes me laugh. I love to blend the visualisation process with strategising on the action steps needed to achieve it… one bite at a time! If it means just rolling your yoga mat out, lacing up your shoes or putting your swimsuit on, just do one thing. One action at a time. Measuring is everything; whenever I take on a new challenge, the first thing I do is get myself a new notebook. This is an excuse to hold a brand new notebook in my hands; usually, Moleskine is my 'go-to' brand. If it's good enough for Picasso, it's good enough for me! I write out my challenge, the time I have available to complete it and divide it down to a realistic timescale. For example, for the Channel swim, it was 2.5 miles a week over three months. Time-wise it was around two-hour-long swimming sessions in the water each week. Squishing it into my schedule took tenacity and discipline - it ruled my life for two months! My first thought of the day, always in the forefront of my mind, was "When am I going to get the lengths in?" and this was the one thought I'd have before anything else. It is constantly on your mind whenever you undertake a challenge, so be aware of that, if it's not, it's perhaps not important enough for you.

Visualising Going to Downing Street

Another picture that was in my visualisation box was that of Number 10 Downing Street, London. I had taken part in the nationwide UK campaign Small Business Saturday for two years, and in the third year, I applied for Small Business 100. The campaign supports small artisan businesses and encourages people to shop small and shop local on the high street. It takes place on the first Saturday in December every year.

One hundred small businesses are featured on each individual day of the 100 days running up to the first of December. I was chosen as one of the hundred, and featured in the press on my day on the 23rd of October. There is a bus tour of the UK, and it happened to start on my day in Dundee, so I went along to meet everyone and had a live interview with the team. I knew that there was a special event taking place at Downing Street, but it was invite-only. I cut out a picture of Downing Street, asked the Universe to help get me there and placed it in my vision box. I would look at it every day and try to visualise myself by the famous black front door, flooding my mind and body with feelings of gratitude as if it had already happened for me.

A few weeks later an email came in, would I like to go to Downing Street? It didn't take long to answer that email I can tell you. A proud moment! Since I was a product-based business, would I also like to have a small stand to display what I do? So I sent 100 small votive candles ahead of myself as a giveaway for the other guests. We had a surreal day; it was such a beautiful and surprisingly comfortable place. I did swan up and down the master staircase a few times with all the eyes of the previous Prime Ministers watching!

You never know who you might meet, so I believe in always treating people the same, regardless of title or wealth or status. Treat everyone like the Queen, and you can't go wrong! Treating everyone with kindness, respect and holding them in high regard opens up doors and opportunities. I love the serendipity of how one event leads to another. At this event at Downing Street, one gentleman claimed his free candle gift, and we got chatting. He had worked there for years looking after each Prime Minister. He gave me his business card and said to give him a shout when I was down with the family.

It wasn't until I was home and realised I was going to be in the vicinity three months later to run the London Half Marathon, which incidentally finished at Downing Street. Now, what a plan that would be if I could get a picture of my friend and myself at Number 10's door with our sponsor charity vests on! I could visualise it quite clearly - I was going to make it happen!

I decided not to tell my friend and have it as a complete surprise; I just had to ensure that she had ID with her, that wasn't going to be too difficult now was it? Until we jumped on the train for the five-hour journey that she realised she forgot her purse - containing ID. Her swift thinking son popped her passport in the post which arrived just in time! She was able to take her passport, and we got our photo taken with our race medals outside Downing Street - all thanks to the connection I had made there at the previous event.

You have to be open to possibilities, and that they won't necessarily come in the form that you think they will, that is why we miss them sometimes, we have to keep our eyes open for any opportunity to arise from anywhere.

I had joined the Female Entrepreneur Association and been a part of the community for a few years when I saw that the founder of the FEA, Carrie Green, was hosting her first party for members. I thought to myself, is it too super indulgent to go to London just for a festive night out at my busiest time of year? Yes definitely! So I put it out to the Universe to take care of it. The thought was out there that I **desired** to go. Well, it just so happened that the party was the evening before the Downing Street event and I would have to be in London the night before. So travelling down on the train while reading Carrie Green's best selling book, She Means Business, there were so many similarities and synchronicities between Carrie and myself. I enjoyed a fabulous night of networking and chatted at Carrie Greens Christmas Party then popped into Downing Street the next morning. It was all meant to be!

Visualising owning a piece of Pippa Small Jewellery

Another thing that I had long desired was a piece of Pippa Small jewellery. She is a wonderful inspirational jeweller who works with women in Kabul. I just adore the rawness of her stunning creations. I could only admire her pieces from afar because the price tag for even the smallest piece was staggeringly expensive - in the thousands of pounds. Not to be deterred, I carried on visualised and desired owning my own piece of Pippa Small jewellery. This time I didn't cut out a picture of the pieces, I just visited her website often! One day in a press article I found whilst scrolling, 'Pippa Small creates affordable pieces of jewellery for Monsoon' oh wowee this IS possible. Well, I must have rung a dozen Monsoon stores. I was like a woman possessed. I was refreshing the websites, looking all over. My tenacity paid off, and I now have a stunning necklace and bracelet in gold and amethyst. These combined cost around £100 compared to the thousands of pounds they are on her website. I couldn't believe it! Keep your eyes open to receiving because it's going to come to you from ways you could never have imagined. I am sharing this with you, not to say look what I have, but look at what YOU could have.

My Son Manifested his Dream Device

I like to teach this same belief of the power of visualisation and manifesting to my son. Last Christmas he said he didn't really want anything and so got lots of smaller bits and bobs and some Air Pods. Coincidentally - not long after Christmas, he lost one of his Air Pods and was really upset about it. I asked the Universe where it was and got a picture in my mind of where to find it. I went straight to the washing machine rubber lip, and there it was!

At the start of the year, he then decided he wanted an iPad Pro and Apple Pencil - a few weeks after Christmas! "Archie, it's just been Christmas, and you already have an iPad why do you need another one?" I asked him. He vowed to sell his current one and said he was going to visualise getting his new iPad and make it happen. I chuckled to myself because I have instilled this in him! I just knew that there was no way I was paying for it - the whole cost of the iPad and Pencil was over £1000!

This seemed like an impossible task for an 11-year-old boy who isn't able to have a regular part-time job. Alas, he was not deterred and in addition to visualising having the iPad in his hands (the 'ask' part) he also devised a plan of HOW he would make it happen (the 'act' part). He offered himself out to all who would accept his help in the form of chopping logs, washing cars, helping his dad at his physio clinic for cleaning equipment. We give him his pocket money on a Friday, and it is relative to how much he has helped around the house. He gets the eggs from the hens, helps light the fire, brings the logs in, hangs out the washing or gets involved in other household tasks.

He started to save every penny he could. He sold toys and things he didn't like or had outgrown. He had a Kilner jar that he was saving all his pounds, pence and notes. It was quite small and starting to fill quickly. "You need a bigger jar," I said to him and knew that making space would help him achieve his goal. I wanted him to understand manifesting.

One of the ways he made the most money was from selling lobsters. In Pittenweem near where we live, we have creels which are small lobster catching baskets. The creel is made from wood and netting and has a weight at the bottom. To entice the lobster into it, you place fish heads in the basket. They crawl into the baskets, but they can't get out. You throw the creel from the rocks into deep water, and it has a buoy on the top, so you know which one is yours. Then when the tide is at its lowest, you walk down and collect your catch. If they're too young, too small or a female lobster with 'berries' which means lobster eggs, then they get thrown back in the sea. Those that make the grade are collected to eat or in Archie's case, to sell.

Archie would sell them for £10 per lobster, and with each catch, he was adding more and more to his Kilner jar of funds to buy his iPad. With only a few weeks to go until his 12th birthday, he was still around £300 short. He wanted to buy himself a cover first so that he could have it in his hands and enhance his visualisation. Next came the pencil which was almost torturous. Every time the postman came, Archie was almost having a heart attack with excitement! By the time his 12th birthday landed, and the fact we were in lockdown due to the pandemic, family and friends could not visit us with gifts, so he was sent so much cash! This would not have happened in normal circumstances, but one good thing about the lockdown for Archie was that it meant he had the funds to get his iPad.

I was so relieved that firstly this was the first time that he had been driven to save money. It is quite difficult to get children to save money, and that delayed gratification is so important for their future development into adulthood. Patience and the importance of saving is so vital and can help children grow up to have a more healthy relationship with money. I was delighted that it was something artistic that he wanted to buy. The iPad has been a source of artistic inspiration for him, and he has been getting to grips with the different digital drawing apps. I felt quite proud, and I did say to him "You're blinking jammy!" that the money had come to him in unexpected circumstances. "What's next? I think I'll manifest a car!" he replied. Even though he's 12, he has decided he wants a Land Rover Defender, so I've told him to start saving now! I think he might need a few of those Kilner jars!

My Outstanding Visualisations

I have a few things I am actively trying to visualise into my life. Some are just a bit of fun and others I am determined to bring to fruition.

Visualising Picking Tea Leaves

Picking tea leaves is something that is on my 'to do' list and again just to reiterate I did not know how or where it would happen, it just would. I am in the field of beautiful lush green leaves, the sun is shining a little through a broken cloud, and the temperature is just beautiful and cool. I have a blue basket tied on my back, and I'm picking tea. Well at least in my head I am, but it is so clear it is like a memory.

I was attending an Annual General Meeting for the first time but part of a group that I am not actively involved in, but I am a member. I hadn't been to any networking events for a long time and knew that I had to get out and do some networking with fellow businesswomen. So I chose the AGM as there would be no 'stand up and introduce yourself' which I am always a bit shy of.

One of the speakers was one of the first-ever tea growers in Scotland! I could not believe my ears! Such an interesting and inspiring talk. I offered my non-existent 'tea leaf' picking skills (although in my head, I was an expert) if she needed.

I'm just looking for a flight in a private jet now! So if you are reading this and have a private jet, I'm asking!

Having a Coutts Bank Account

I have cut out a picture of a Coutts bank card and put it into my purse. I have also downloaded the app on my phone, which makes my husband laugh because it says "Access denied" every time I try to log in. When I went to London, I even stopped off outside the building and got a selfie there. People normally go to London to get a selfie at Big Ben or Trafalgar Square, and there's me pointing my camera phone at my face in front of Coutts!

Yet before you think I'm totally bonkers, having the fake card and the app is a sign of earning a particular amount of money for me. So I like to think of Coutts as my business success and growth. Customers need at least £500,000 in cash or £5m in assets to open an account. Coutts is the official bank of the Queen. Although I can't see her splashing out on Amazon prime orders, can you?

Sailing Around the World

By now, after reading this book, you will know that I love to travel. There is something I would love to do with my family, and that is to travel around the world by boat. I once found an article in the back of a travel brochure about an around the world cruise. It had a list of places that you would visit around the globe. I cut this out and created a special book. For example, the first place on the list was Antigua. I went on Tripadvisor and researched the top three things to do in Antigua and wrote about them in my book. I continued that for all the destinations on the list. I know that when we do eventually go, I have a ready-made itinerary!

I want to go Southampton to Southampton. I don't want to fly; I want to travel UK soil to UK soil. I live by the sea every day, and I think if I hopped on that ocean right now, it would take me around the world. I like to visualise myself on the ship, waving goodbye to Southampton full of excitement for the journey ahead. I estimate it will take us three months and I have already stalked all the websites, picked my cabin and half-packed my imaginary holiday wardrobe. I have a notebook which has a list of the trip destinations, and I have added the top 3 Trip Advisor recommendations in each destination.

Going to Necker Island

Another picture that sits in my vision box is a picture of Necker Island. I saw a picture in a travel magazine of a floating lunch with sushi, and I thought "That's for me! I want to be there!" This has been in my vision box for a while. To keep it in my focus and continue my visualisation practice, I go onto the website frequently, and I am on their newsletter. I go on the website and think "Which room would I like?" "What sports would Archie do?" I have even gone as far as to research the flights and the airport transfers. I really do think it will happen!

I once had a meeting with a local luxury hotel about creating their own private label candles. Speaking to the manager, I learned that she had once been the manager at Necker Island! I told her all about my dream to go and asked if she thought Richard Branson would like some Necker Island private label candles. Sadly, since the island was struck by lightning and had a serious fire, no candles are allowed! I will have to get my thinking cap on and tap into my manifesting magic to make it happen. Maybe I will stop there on my round the world boat trip? Who knows.

Play the Manifesting Game

This is an exciting game to play with yourself, like-minded friends or your children. You may have heard people talking about seeing spiritual numbers like 11:11 and 22:22 well here is a way to gamify that and put it into manifesting practice. Some believe that seeing 111 is a sign that angelic beings are close by.

In the book *Raise Your Vibration: 111 Practices to Increase Your Spiritual Connection* by Kyle Gray, I found a great piece on signs, and you can try it today. I see signs of 11 or 11.11 everywhere and the more in tune I am, the more I see it. I sometimes have to laugh. I see it so often. So I decided to have a game with my son who could spot it first.

On this one particular occasion, we were on the way to a running race that he wanted to take part in. I explained all the obvious places you might spot it, house numbers, car registrations, on the digital clock or your phone. I got him to actively ask to see the signs and be open to the Universe, demonstrating the numbers before him. Before long we were in full swing looking for places where 111 could be. "Mum look the petrol is £1.11!" he squealed, and his little face lit up with wonder and excitement.

When we arrived at the race destination, I parked up while he went to get registered and get his race number. He came running over with the biggest widest grin, waving his arms and pointing to the number attached to his chest. Guess what number it was? You guessed it - 111. Thankfully he didn't come 111th in the race!

I am also a firm believer in divine messages, the more I meditate, the more in tune I become. When either the face of someone pops into my head or a word or place which might seem a bit out of the ordinary I stop and think "What is the message?" I occasionally just stop the car and Google or call the person. I'm not a fan of Elvis but his song 'Now or never' is incredibly poignant, I truly believe in acting on impulse and acting straight away. I believe these fleeting thoughts are messages that we should act on.

Play the Money Manifesting Game

If you don't know how much things cost, then how can they be in your realm? Money mindset courses will teach you that in order to manifest money, you need to know what you will spend it on. That's why I love to spend time manifesting and researching prices of Necker Island holidays or tea picking trips or travelling around the world by boat. If you know what kind of lifestyle your desire will cost you, you will be able to visualise it happening and take the right action steps to get there.

If you'd like to learn more about manifesting for yourself, but you don't know where to start, here are some ideas for you;

Vision Board

One way of bringing what you want to life is by creating a vision board. There are many places that do fun workshops on this, or you can do it at home. It is a good game to play with children too. The idea is you get large A3 pieces of card, a lot of magazines or newspapers, take some scissors and glue and go through the publications to see if anything jumps out at you that you could put on your vision board. If you have something specific like a piece of jewellery, a brand of car, holiday destination etc. then you could print out those specific pictures and add those to your vision board. Although I find that these things I desire usually appear in the magazines as if by magic.

On my own vision board, I always leave some blank space to let in what I have not yet visualised. I feel that it leaves room for a wild card. You just never know what is around the corner.

Online Vision Board

One of my friends doesn't like having a vision board out for everyone to see as it is personal to her, so she has created a vision board on Trello. Trello is a card-based organisation software programme and app and my friend has downloaded pictures of the things she wants to be, do and have and logs into the board and looks at it every morning as part of her visualisation practice. She has also collated a few of the things on her digital board into one image that is her phone wallpaper and computer screensaver.

Vision Box

This is my preferred method. I like having a vision box of things I can touch and feel. In my vision box at present are things like a picture of a private jet, a beautiful pink house I have seen and fallen in love with, Buckingham Palace and my Necker Island, boat trip and tea picking holiday pictures.

I like having items I can hold and feel in my hands, so the vision box works well.

Tarot/Medium/Oracle Cards

Some people consult more spiritual ways of manifesting by calling in the help of a medium, spiritualist or using tarot or oracle cards. Tarot cards are usually reserved for those who believe themselves to be spiritual, psychic or have medium abilities. Oracle cards can be whatever the person who created the cards wants. You can get oracle cards in a multitude of designs, and they are usually accompanied by a guide book to give some additional affirmations or meanings. A friend recently purchased some oracle cards for me, so I have been reading the accompanying book and may use the cards in my daily meditation practice.

Manifestation Meditation

Meditation is a powerful tool to change your mental state, bring clarity into your life and relax. There are specific manifestation meditation tracks available on different platforms, including the one I use - Insight Timer. You can also download and listen to many meditation manifesting tracks for free. There is an American girl who goes by the name Manifestation Babe who provides a lot of free content online on manifesting.

Affirmations

Repeating affirmations can be another part of the manifesting process. Believing yourself to be, do or have something before it has happened and state that fact out loud to yourself is very powerful. Using affirmations like "I am a world record holder" or "I am a millionaire" as part of an affirmation process can help you ask for what you want to be, do and have.

How to Manifest Your Dream Business

I touch on this in Chapter 7, Being Brave but don't be scared to ask for what you want in your business both to the Universe and to others.

If you need help, ask for it. Put it out there to the Universe to guide you to the right person or mentor or solution that will help get you growing your business. I have done this a lot for those who have helped me on my business journey.

When I launched my online Candlemaking Made Easy digital course, my studio was closed due to COVID19, so I asked the Universe for help. I realised in a flash of inspiration that I could record my beginner's candle making workshop and sell it online in a digital course format. This would mean I could still generate some kind of income during the pandemic. I got everything laid out in my kitchen and filmed it all using my iPhone. I filmed 12 individual videos in one sitting and spoke just like I was doing a workshop. It isn't perfect, but it was more important to get it out there quickly than worrying about making it perfect and delaying its release.

Be brave in asking for what you want, and then you will be more likely to take the relevant action associated with it. Let's say you have a desire to increase your followers to a certain amount. If you visualise that happening, you are more likely to then feel confident enough to follow through with the right action in terms of showing up online, nurture your audience and be consistent with your content.

If you have a specific sales goal that you want to manifest then visualise it happening. Yes, you might feel excited at the number on your bank balance, but that image of achieving that number will drive you to make those extra sales calls, work on making your pitch better, increase your connections or sell a new product. The feeling that visualisation gives you is one of gratitude which in turn drives excitement, possibility and motivation. When you feel it, and you feel like you already have it, you just have to join the dots backwards to make it happen.

Letter from the Future Exercise

This is a popular exercise in self-development. Write a letter to yourself from the future you, can download the template in the workbook. You can use a website resource called Future Me, and they will send the letter to you at a certain point in the future.

Always address the letter to yourself and focus on being grateful.

This would be an example of a letter from your future self:

I am so happy and grateful that I am now fully qualified in Mandarin, that we have a beautiful home in the south of France with sea views and a private pool. I'm glad I took the decision to pursue sailing, and we now have a fabulous yacht in the harbour. I stuck with that diet that I was on and am happy in my skin having released the two stone of additional body fat I didn't need! Archie has settled into the University of his first choice to study engineering astrophysics with a dream of being an astronaut and being part of the SpaceX program. Our round the world circumnavigation by boat was a huge success being made better with an upgrade to a suite with a private butler. My donations to the Woodland Trust has now seen over a million trees being planted in Scotland. I completed my Wim Hof Training and now run retreat weekends in Scotland. I currently run annual Empower Women retreats in Scotland, bringing women from all over the world together to learn new skills from over 30 practitioners in meditation, holistic therapies, yoga, aromatherapy and Reiki.

I did this exercise years ago before I even had a child, but one of the lines in the letter says I'm glad my child has settled into (the very school he is at now). I know that not everything will come true but remember the first stage in manifesting is writing something down.

Exercise: Ask & Act

Pick something from this chapter to help you strengthen your manifesting practice:

1. Create a vision board or a vision box with your desires for your life and business
2. Write a list of 100 things to be, do or have as per the workbook which accompanies this book. Download yours at www.jomacfarlane.com/bonus
3. Write a letter to yourself from your future self where you're thankful and grateful for all you have achieved. Write in the letter how everything has been brought to fruition and how it has made you feel and impacted your life.

Chapter 7

Be Brave

"Courage is like a muscle. We strengthen it with use."

- Ruth Gordon

If I had to give you one piece of advice when setting up your own business, it would be to develop courage, tenacity and grit; aka you need to **be brave**.

In the words of Elizabeth Gilbert of Eat Pray Love "The universe buries strange jewels deep within us all, and then stands back to see if we can find them".

Think about any big business success story from the last century. They have all come with an element of risk. From Henry Ford creating the very first motorcar to Steve Jobs creating Apple and Richard Branson creating his many business brands in so many sectors. Each one required the business leader to be brave, have courage, tenacity and grit.

Setting up a new business is always risky. Often, people will leave the security and comfort of their 9-5 corporate careers and decide to follow a dream and start their big goal of creating their own business. There is something so wonderful and amazing about the blood, sweat and tears that goes into setting up, establishing and continuing to drive your own business. You will probably work longer and harder than ever before, but get it right and growing your own business will be the most rewarding thing you ever do.

There will be times when you feel desperate, without any idea of what to do for the best and worried that your business will fail. If you think about it, if you have had a full-time career at some point in your life, you will have been a cog in an overall machine. Maybe you worked in sales, or maybe you worked in administration. Maybe you were a manager. When you work as part of a bigger business, you play your own individual role as part of a bigger picture. When you set up your own business you will do this out of a personal desire and drive to create something that is important to you. Often, when starting off in a new business it is your passion to bring your message or product to the world or a financial drive that is the fuel for your entrepreneurial endeavour. One thing you might not anticipate when you start your journey is how many hats you will need to wear in the beginning. When you start your business it will be to birth your product or service into the world. All of a sudden you will realise that you have to also get good at all the other bits too - the finances, the marketing, the manufacturing. Sometimes these are things we have absolutely no idea about! When you've worked in a corporate role and been a part of a business, you have looked after your own department and day to day tasks. Suddenly you have your own business and ALL those tasks fall on your shoulders. That is why I stressed earlier in the book the importance of never stop learning.

This is part of your life now as a business owner - to learn, to grow both personally and professionally and to continue to drive your business.

This will require you to be brave so many times. You will get overwhelmed and stressed out about things that are not in your area of expertise. You will make mistakes. You will make decisions based on what you know already, not what might be the right answer for your business. You will hopefully grow to a level where you're able to get support and advice from a coach or a programme that expands your skills and knowledge. That's exactly the reason why I created my own Ignite Your Creativity 12-week programme to bring your business into fruition and make it a reality. I don't want you to have to go through the hardships and the learning that I went through in order to bring my business to fruition. I wanted to share with you all the pitfalls and tips, tricks and hacks I could muster that would mean you have a clear roadmap to follow and you will not need to go through the craziness of setting up your own business alone.

You'll grow and be able to take on staff which brings a whole new element of bravery as you hand over the reins of some aspects of your business to the responsibility of someone else.

You will second guess yourself, doubt yourself, question yourself and wonder why the heck you started this damn business in the first place. I promise you that with consistent effort, the right support continued learning and courage that you CAN be a business success. As previously mentioned it is important when you hit a plateau in your business that you keep on going. Don't change your goal but you might have to change the way you approach it. I have given up on a few things in my life when I hit a plateau and I wonder what would have happened if I hadn't. As the quote goes 'It's always darkest just before the dawn'.

Setting out in business can be terrifying as much as it is exciting, but isn't that the same with anything in life? Knowledge is power and once you collect knowledge you will increase in confidence as you learn new skills and adapt.

When Have You Had Courage?

If you are ever having a day in your business where you doubt yourself and your abilities in any aspect of growing your business, take a step back and think about the times in your life when you have been brave. Think back to those times where you have had courage, tenacity and grit and how it worked out for you. It doesn't have to be centred around business either, this could be any event in your life.

One story of mine that comes to mind is the day I climbed the Forth Bridge in Scotland. My husband came home from a charity golf day having won a prize in the raffle. It was for a guided trip up to the top of the Forth Bridge. I knew that this was a very rare experience as there is no official viewing platform for the public on the bridge. So before my head had a chance to instil some fear, my Scottish heart cried "How exciting! Wow! Amazing! Yes!"

To set the scene, if you're unfamiliar with the Forth Bridge in Scotland, it is the iconic red bridge to the west of central Edinburgh. The Forth Bridge is considered a symbol of Scotland having been voted Scotland's greatest man-made wonder in 2016, and it is a UNESCO World Heritage site. The bridge links Fife to Edinburgh and also carries the Edinburgh to Aberdeen train line. It is 8,094 feet or

2,467m long and 360 feet or 10 metres high. The bridge, being so well-loved and iconic, has plans for an official visitors viewing platform and a walk, much like the Sydney Harbour bridge walks that have been operational for many years. However, the 130-year-old bridge has only ever welcomed a handful of normal everyday folk to the top of the bridge to see out across the waters.

It had been in all the papers about the opportunity to go to the top of the bridge. It was a very rare occurrence and tickets had been released to charities across Scotland to raffle or sell off to raise funds for their charitable causes and give people this once in a lifetime opportunity. I should point out that I am absolutely terrified of heights! But I wanted to see those unbeatable 360-degree views of my home country and stand on the iconic bridge that I had loved and looked at my entire life. I had only ever seen the steel imposing structures of the red Forth Bridge through the windows of the moving train as we passed over the bridge to get to Edinburgh, or from the car on the nearby road bridge. I wanted to see that alternative perspective - I just had to get over my fear first!

The weather on the day of the bridge climb was awful so I was worried my panic-stricken efforts would not be worth the promised panoramic uninterrupted views of the Edinburgh and Fife coastline.

I arrived at the meeting point at the bottom of the legs of the bridge at 9:30nam promptly and wondered what the hell I was doing. The choppy waters underneath the bridge were like muddy sludge and the sky was grey. The white horse crest of the waves seemed to gallop for miles and even on the ground level, the wind was whistling in my ears.

Only a few thousand people have ever been to the top of the bridge including those who constructed the bridge 130 years ago, the continued maintenance team and the painters. The phrase "It was like painting the Forth Bridge" is a common expression in Scotland because the bridge is that long people used to think that the painting was a never-ending cyclical job. So painters, structural engineers, Network Rail representatives and a handful of the competition winning or charity fundraising people had been the only ones to grace the bridge's majestic top. I don't know why I was surprised to see that we would be making our ascent using a tiny rickety elevator. This was not a tourist attraction activity. There was no specially created and constructed visitors centre, safety equipment or harnesses to wear. Oh no. It was just me and a few other people, gradually rising to the top of the bridge while the wind howled with more force with every metre we climbed. My heartbeat threatened to deafen us all as the muddy brown water and the trains below shrunk in size before my eyes.

When at the top of the elevator we were encouraged to walk out onto a viewing platform. As I said, no harnesses just a few of us on the top. We did wear hard hats but I worried they would swoop off our heads with one gust of wind.

Some people headed to the edge of the platform and took a good look down (crazy people!) Others posed for selfies and seemed to have to counterbalance their weight against what felt like gale-force winds to get the angle just right. Others oohed and ahhed and pointed out landmarks and views across the horizon. Me? I stood fixed to the middle of the platform not daring to step another step towards those dangerous-looking rickety sides. I felt like my core muscles were made of steel rods as I attempted to mentally mould myself to the middle of that platform. In other words, I was absolutely shitting myself. I don't think I have ever been as terrified in my whole life. I'd love to give you the Hollywood version of this story and tell you that I had a word with myself, sorted out my fear and went and got my photo at the edge but that would be lying. I couldn't bring myself to do it and almost fainted with relief when the guide told us it was time to head back to the rickety elevator and head back down. The relief of the return journey allowed me to look out across the horizon and see the spectacular view as the red steel structure flashed before me and we got back down to ground level.

I sat in my car a while after returning. My adrenaline still flooded my veins making me feel a heightened sense of elation that I was safe and back on the Earth's solid ground. As I placed my still shaking hands on the steering wheel and let out a sharp exhale, I felt a sense of pride. I had done it. I had felt the fear but done it anyway. I had come out of my comfort zone and achieved what I would've thought was unthinkable. There are plans for a visitor centre and proper bridge climb and viewing platform to be constructed on the Forth Bridge in the next few years. I know that I will be able to go back there with my family again one day and that climb next time will feel so much easier and achievable. Who knows? Maybe I will even go to the edges this time! The point is that confidence and being brave comes with practice practice practice. We often build up an event in our minds before we have even experienced it in reality. Often, our thoughts around things are the fear rather than the event itself.

You will have many times when you have overcome a fear or the negative effects of the thoughts of a fear. Learning to bottle that feeling of getting out of your own way and doing it anyway will stand you in good stead in your business endeavours. I know when I came back from my bridge climb that I did feel like anything was possible. It's like the adrenaline rush had given me a gift in realising that overcoming the feeling of fear brought an even greater emotion on the other side of it. It is that feeling of achievement and accomplishment, pride and happiness that fuels the next brave decision you have to make. Sometimes you just need reminding that you have got the capability and experience to push past your fears. (Check out the exercise at the end of this chapter for more on this).

Taking a Risk

The definition of risk is: 'To try and do something for which there is a high probability of a negative or unfortunate outcome.'

I personally think there are two types of risk - one which you have control over and the other where you are putting the risk in the hands of another. If you think about someone doing a parachute jump, the element of risk doesn't just come from jumping from a great height out of an aeroplane. There are elements out of your control: "Did he attach my parachute straps tightly enough as I step towards the door of the aircraft door at 13,000ft?"

Some risks are not able to be predicted and you put your trust in others only to be let down. Like the time I put my trust in a driver in Ghana to take us safely to our hotel after a long flight. Our driver tipped off some muggers and our bus was attacked. The driver ran off, leaving us vulnerable like sitting ducks. It was a terrifying experience and one that could've easily caused mental and emotional trauma, leaving me wanting to quit my career in travel. While it was one of the most horrid experiences of my life, I chose to learn from it and move on. It made me more vigilant in the future and trust my gut more in unfamiliar scenarios.

On a daily basis, we risk our lives in the hands of others. Is that driver going to stay on their side of the road as they text their friend? Will my surgeon bring me back around from my operation? There are just different degrees of risk in life and just because there is a risk, it should not stop you from at least exploring your options and deciding whether or not to try something in your life or business. Just because there's an element of danger or potential negative outcome, does that mean you must stay safe and secure in a personal bubble? Michelangelo once said, "The greater danger for most of us lies not in setting our aim too high and falling short, but setting our aim too low and achieving our mark."

Sometimes life is about risking everything for a dream no one can see but you. That is so true for many of the people I meet looking to start and grow their own business. If it is out of the ordinary of what people may have expected of you, it can be difficult to convey how much it means to you and why you're working so hard on it. Having belief and a desire to see things through to fruition will hopefully see you make your business a success. Be prepared to put in the hard work and for others not to realise your end goal as clear as you do. You really have to trust your heart and hope that those around you will support your decisions.

I had a nervous breakdown prior to 1993 working over 70 hours a week with three jobs in advertising, waitressing and for SKY at the same time. I couldn't drive and had endless panic attacks and the situation got so bad, my dad flew off his oil rig and he and my mum came down to Berkshire to bring me home to Scotland. It was a slow and painful road going from burned out and broken down to feeling like me again. I eventually settled back into working as a waitress. A few months later, I decided to try for a career in air travel and was offered the job with British Midland. In the interview, I was crushed to learn that the job would not be based out of Edinburgh as I initially expected. The job would be based in Heathrow. Which would mean more time travelling for me. I was worried. I'd broken apart doing those crazy hours once before and was worried I would not cope again. I'm not sure if this was being brave, taking a risk or just knowing in my heart that it was the right thing to do and knowing from experience that I would be armed with the mental tools to avoid a breakdown again, I took the role. My heart told me this was the right thing to do. I went on to apply for British Airways and work on the 'beach fleet' out of Gatwick flying to the likes of Antigua, Seychelles, Barbados and Bermuda then I flew out of Heathrow which led to destinations like Hong Kong, Buenos Aires and Sydney. All of these experiences completely shaped my life and I often wonder what my life would've been like had I not accepted that job and taken what was a risk at the time. Unfortunately, we don't all get to see our lives played out like Gwyneth Paltrow in the film Sliding Doors, so we have to be happy in our decisions, risks, the time we had courage and the times we were brave.

The Biology of Risk

Taking a risk isn't for everyone, it is apparently linked to the amygdala, (maybe I should have mine scanned) the walnut-sized part of the brain linked to fear and emotions. It takes in information, processes it and sends signals to your adrenal glands to secrete adrenaline.

I watched the film Free Solo recently which depicts the risks Alex

Honnold took to free climb El Capitan, a granite monolith in Yosemite a height of 3,600ft. With years of practice and planning down to mapping the tiniest of toe and finger holes, he achieved his dream in 2017 in less than four hours. What was interesting is that they studied his brain, they gave him an MRI scan and studied his reaction to shocking images and found that his amygdala was almost impossible to stimulate. Which would explain his aversion to risk. With the amygdala not stimulated, the usual biological signals were not sent to other parts of his body and he effectively had no fear.

The Fear of Risk in Business

For the rest of us, the fear of taking a risk can either work as a good motivator to get out of our comfort zone, or it can keep us well and truly stuck.

Taking a risk sometimes requires us to realise that it is only us standing in our way and the excuses we make act as a false fear. We can get caught up in striving for perfection, making our situation risk-averse, when in actual fact the reality of what happens is you end up procrastinating on making any kind of decision that will propel you into action.

In my own business, I had a huge perceived fear of releasing my candles without a particular box. I know this sounds very dramatic but it was really holding me back. By this point I'd been candle making for four years without boxes, selling them from home or at Christmas fairs, night markets or events at luxury hotels. One day I decided that the key to growing my business was providing my candles in boxes. They would look better and be better presented. They would look more expensive and I could charge more for them. I was so stuck in indecision about what sort of style the box needed to be in order to look more professional. I had to order a minimum amount of boxes to get the best price and almost recoiled in fear as I realised I would need to order 300 boxes. It was the biggest order I had needed to do in my business to date and it made me realise this was an actual business. Not a hobby, or a pastime. This was my business and I was going to invest £700 on my 300 boxes and be in a position to approach luxury hotels and more high-end stockists.

I remained stuck on this for months. I was so indecisive and I ended up wasting hours online researching the perfect materials, textures and styles. By chance, at the Tony Robbins firewalk event I had attended, I met a brilliant coach called Jacob Melaard. We stayed in touch after the firewalk and knowing that I was feeling out of line and out of sorts but couldn't put my finger on what was wrong, I arranged a Zoom coaching call session with him. He lives in Dubai and used Zoom to deliver his sessions in all things mindset coaching and his speciality technique called EFT - Emotional Freedom Technique which I hadn't heard of before. It involves tapping your fingers lightly on eight points on the face and body which works like acupuncture and affects the energy of your body. Well, I love anything like this and so gave it a go. I was shocked but not surprised to hear his feedback after working together. Jacob made me realise after coaching that I was scared to launch and was hiding under the guise of not being able to find the perfect box. I was putting myself in situations which made it hard for me to launch on purpose. Launching would mean having to focus on marketing and social media along with sales. These were not areas of expertise that were familiar to me. Growing my business would also mean taking me to the next level, investing in premises and moving my business from kitchen table to bona fide workshop. It wasn't the boxes that were holding me back, it was my fear of growth. My fear of taking a risk and growing the business. This is exactly what I had dreamed about so how could this have manifested for me? On further coaching sessions with Jacob, I identified that I was scared of everyone's judgement. Even people that did not matter to me or the growth of my business. I was stuck in stories of what people might say about me or might think. I was scared of making money and worried people might say "Who does she think she is?" Sometimes people in my village can be a bit mean and I'd heard lots of conversations over the years that centred on tearing people down rather than bumping them up. I realised that this did not have to be my own personal truth and hiding behind ordering boxes was stopping my dreams of growing my business dead in its tracks.

Les Brown has a great quote that I'd like you to remember for these future scenarios where you worry about what others will think of your business endeavours and you as a person:

'Other people's opinions of you does not define you.'

This was a really good lesson in risk-taking in business for me. It wasn't the biggest risk in ordering 300 boxes and the worst outcome would be that I would lose £700 if I didn't go on to sell the candles in boxes. It taught me about the power that perfectionism can have over us and it gave me the strength and courage to challenge myself when perfectionism strikes. It is never me wanting things to be perfect, it is usually rooted in me fearing I will fail or worrying what others will think of me. I don't strive for perfection because I know it doesn't exist anymore, it's far more important to get your product or yourself out there than creating long drawn out situations that are preventing you from moving forward. Sometimes, you just have to get out of your own way.

There is a quote I love - 'Failing is learning' and I repeat it often. Although this came to bite me on the backside when my son was heading into his Grade 2 Piano exam. He said, "Failing is good, remember you said, mum!". Oops. Well son, maybe not right this second and certainly not what his wonderfully patient piano teacher would want to hear! However, there is beauty in not being afraid to fail. Fail fast and fail often. You will always learn from it.

The Fear of Visibility in Business

In a modern-day small business, most of us have some form of social media presence. I always say that people buy people. Customers like to know the faces behind products, services and brands. For me, my business is me and my name so I have no choice but to be me and stand in my power demonstrating who I am, what I stand for and how my business can help people. But even doing things like going live on Facebook or putting an image out there of yourself and your product on social media can feel incredibly daunting and risky to some people. The fear of what other people will think and say or your own feelings about your appearance or your perfectionism will stop you from showing up, being visible and promoting your business.

You might have been through this yourself. There might have been something you thought about doing in your business, but didn't go for it and take the risk at the time. Maybe you stalled on hiring someone to help you and tried to do absolutely everything in your business from accounts to marketing, sales to spreadsheets. One day you realise you will need to invest some of your profits back into getting the professional help you need. Once you've taken the risk and you realise it has freed up valuable resources - particularly in your own personal energy, you will wish you had done it earlier and not been put off because you thought it was too risky.

Try a Power Pose

Now you might laugh at this but there is science that backs this up. You could power pose your way into taking risks, feeling brave and having courage. A power pose is where you use your body positioning to stand up firm, tall and strong. Think Wonder Woman with hands-on hips, chin high and chest upwards. Check out Amy Cuddy's talk on TED Talks, she is a social psychologist at Harvard Business school who explores the role of body language in how we feel, think and act. By standing in this way, tall, chest out hands-on hips has been shown to decrease stress hormones by up to 25% according to Cuddy. Animals do it in nature too so we can learn from the animal kingdom when it comes to approaching risk and boosting confidence. I notice this in my own garden often and it makes me smile seeing the power pose demonstrated by my own hens. As I live on the coast, we have a lot of seagulls overhead. When seagulls approach our hens the funny feathered ladies suddenly have the ability to walk on their tiptoes and double their size by fluffing out their feathers. They're quite clearly demonstrating their own power pose. When human beings stand in a series of power poses, it increases your testosterone and reduces cortisol, the stress hormone. Now you don't have to stand in the boardroom or in the middle of your shop or the middle of your office in front of people and do these power poses. You can do them in private to start your day off on the right foot and feel strong and courageous. If you are about to enter an interview you could pop to the loo beforehand and adopt a power pose. If you're happy doing them in public - go for it! Why not! I used to do it at the start of a race or before I made a telephone call so I shifted my energy and felt strong and ready.

I discovered an interesting fact when researching risk-taking and the development of a child's brain. When children are allowed to take risks, it helps their brain development and turns them into well rounded healthy analytical adults. As a parent myself, I find this a harder pill to swallow in practice than in theory. When my son was four, I watched in horror as my husband gave him a sledgehammer to take out a fireplace during our home renovation! He also learned from a young age to light a fire, whittle with a penknife and chop the logs for the fire with his own axe. All of which are risky and make me feel incredibly uncomfortable but the more learning I have done on neuroscience over my years of devouring books, the more I understand that this is a necessary part of him growing up and his brain developing.

Increasing Your Courage and Confidence on a Daily Basis

When starting out in business, I understand it can be an unnerving time. Knowledge is power and until you add to your knowledge through experience, learning or being coached/mentored, you can feel anxious, scared and uncomfortable. There are small things that you can do on a daily basis to help increase your confidence. I can only share with you my own list and these things take time to understand and test for yourself in your own situation. These are my confidence-boosting must-haves:

1. I always carry Rescue Remedy with me and know if I have a busier day than normal or in the past when I'd have a hectic

flight, I'd take a couple of drops and the flight would be a breeze.

2. If you have a difficult task to do, visualise it in your head like a movie running and having the desired outcome so when you come to do it, it actually feels like you have already been there. Napoleon Hill said, "if you can see it in your head you can hold it in your hand".

3. Smile more often. Smiling reduces the stress hormones and increases hormones like oxytocin responsible for feelings of love and happiness.

4. Exercise daily - 20 minutes a day has been shown to increase confidence.

5. Make small steps towards a bigger one - want to take a trip of a lifetime? Start by researching destinations, travel companies, Trip Advisor on what to do when you are there and you will feel like you are almost living it already. Want to sign up for that art, cookery or flower arranging course you have been wanting to do or maybe there is a sport you have always wanted to try? Look into your options and make a commitment to yourself that you will at least enquire about joining.

6. Simple things like having your hair done or wearing clothes that make you feel good can boost your self-confidence. Or making a commitment to do the things that make you feel good like I mentioned in Chapter 2 - Feel Good. That might be wearing great shoes that make you walk more upright and feel more confident. It might be investing in pieces of clothing that really flatter your shape. It might be committing to putting on makeup or doing your hair each morning.

7. Speak with confidence but don't talk to fill gaps. When I failed at one of the many job interviews I have been to, I'd talk until they had to interrupt me with the next question. I learned to answer and stay quiet, that way the ball goes back into their court. Listening is a skill. Sometimes when you do rabbit on with your words, people can see it for what it is - nervousness. Learn to get comfortable with the silence.

Trust Your Gut

In life and business, I am a firm believer that you should always trust your gut. I didn't do this recently and it caused so much stress. I had been looking for a company to etch my candle glasses in gold rather than printed labels. I wanted to be able to offer my high-end private label clients this option and spent a lot of time researching companies that offered this service. I struggled to find many places in the UK but found a specialist in Birmingham. I was delighted I would be able to get this done on home soil and expected the process to take a couple of months. I struggled to liaise with the company right from the start and should've trusted my gut there and then. I shipped off 500 of my beautiful glass vessels ready to be etched in gold and waited. And waited and waited and waited. Email communication was ignored and any phone correspondence resulted in me being passed from pillar to post. The delay in receiving the glasses back caused embarrassment with my private label clients and I worried my investment in the glass and the etching would be lost. Finally, over a whole YEAR after placing the original order, my candle glasses arrived. The quality of the etching was substandard and I realised I had only been sent around 420 glasses - there were 80 glasses missing! I was told on the phone that they allow this for contingency but it was just not good enough! I had lost 16% of my stock to this company.

I should've trusted my gut and I didn't. The knock-on effect of the stress this has caused me has made me quite angry - mainly at myself for not listening to my inner instincts which are so important to me. I am a big believer in energy and the power of energy being aligned or misaligned. I am a fan of quantum mechanics and quantum energy - I can't get enough of the teachings of this phenomenon and really understand the power of someone or a company being on your wavelength or your vibe. This time I didn't listen or honour the familiar feeling of my energy not quite flowing right. Trust the niggle. It is not usually wrong!

Be Brave and Set Boundaries

Having no formal qualification in Art meant it was tricky getting into galleries but I decided to be brave and calculate how I could approach it. I had been accepted to art college when I was younger but I took a job in an Advertising Agency instead. I knew that if I got into the Art Institutes open exhibitions the RSW, RGI, PAI and RSA then that would gain me some recognition and so it did. It wasn't easy, I spent a good deal of time studying what other artists that were getting into these annual exhibitions were doing, not so much their style of painting, more which artists were getting into each gallery. If you have heard of Pareto's law, which states that 80% of effects come from 20% of causes, I applied this thinking to art and realised that only 20% of an artist's success was down to artistic skill and 80% came down to having the guts to just take that step, do it and get your art out there. There are definitely way more talented artists than me but I was brave and took the courage to pursue what I desired. I have learned to get comfortable with someone telling me no, I don't take it personally or let it stop me and my momentum, I just move on.

After meeting a few artists at exhibitions and quizzing them on who their framer was, a name repeatedly came up. I found Allan Black of Artists Surfaces. I call him a framer 'to the stars' as he creates the most creamy delicious frames (no other way of describing it) for a lot of Scotland's most famous artists. I couldn't afford his frames, but I drove to Glasgow to meet him and see if I could persuade him to make me the smallest frame that I could afford - just and probably the smallest he has ever made!

Painting inserted into my new frames I was accepted into the RSW at the Mound in Edinburgh and then into the PAI (Paisley Art Institute) then the RGI (Royal Glasgow Institute) and the other galleries followed. It was quite an odd and slightly stressful situation, dropping your painting off for it then to be paraded in front of judges. Then wait patiently on the yes/no email to say whether you got in, cry in your paint if it didn't – then return to pick it up. Quite often the frames would get damaged so it could be an expensive experience.

When you own and operate your own business you will need to be brave and set boundaries. I have to admit that I am better at this now than I used to be. When you're setting up your business and there are lots of initial outlays to pay for, you do tend to go the extra mile to get the sales in and break even or get into profit. It is the normal business journey but there do need to be some boundaries and balance between home and business. I talk about this in more depth in Chapter 9, Master the Work-Life Challenge.

Having the courage to say no, no thank you and no thanks are important phrases in business. People will try and take advantage of you. People will disrespect your time. If you don't set your schedule your customers will. People will complain. Having the strength of character and conviction to stand by your morals, your values and your beliefs and say no is vital for your business and your own personal self-care. You don't need to do this in a negative way, you can still outline your boundaries with kindness.

One example I can give you with this from my own business perspective is the challenge I have with charitable causes. Because I create luxury goods I am often asked to donate my goods to charitable causes. Unfortunately, there are so many charity causes, you can't possibly donate to them all. I realised this early on in my business that it was very very difficult to say no. I came up with a solution to nominate a dedicated charity that my business would support and crafted a response for the many requests that I get for charity approaches. I focused on the one dedicated charity and gave 10% of my profits away to my chosen cause. That way I felt a sense of pride that I was able to support a worthwhile cause, but I also have the boundaries to be able to say no and explain why I can't support everyone.

I created my Ignite Your Creativity course as a way to monetise my experience in business, share all I have learned and do it in a way that I am financially compensated for my time. I am a firm believer in there being enough business for everyone and I am happy to mentor those looking to create a candle making business. This course was created as a direct result of the many questions and queries that would come to me about setting up in business. I spent almost a year developing the course and modules to give people the best tools possible to create their own creative business. It now means that any time someone wants to "pick my brains" about creating their own candle making business, I can offer them a spot on my coaching and mentoring programme which is the best option for them and also protects my time, knowledge, expertise and my inbox.

Chapter 8

Be Kind

"True kindness lies with the act of giving without the expectation of something in return."

- Katharine Hepburn

They say that kindness is infectious. This is why it is so vital that we talk to ourselves in a positive and kind manner. Our self-talk is the only thing we truly have any control over. What we think and say to ourselves is often the most important voice we need to hear. Our words also have the power to influence those around us and even plants!

The Effect of Our Words on Plants

You may have seen that IKEA did a PR campaign in 2018 encouraging children to bully a plant and see the effect of unkind words on the plant's structure and growth potential. Both plants were placed in schools across the United Arab Emirates and each had a speaker in the container in which they sat. One had a speaker that repeated negative and 'bully' words while the other had loving-kindness and gratitude and compliments bestowed on it. Within a few weeks, students could quite clearly see the effects of the words on both plants, The one that had been 'bullied' was wilted and droopy. The leaves had changed colour. Whereas the plant that received positive compliments was lush, tall, deep green and thriving. This was an important message for the students who witnessed this experiment in real-time over the course of the weeks the plants were placed in their schools. It reminded students of the power of their words.

I always think of these experiments when I catch my inner critic speaking to myself in a way that is overly harsh, critical or negative. I think it is so important to talk to ourselves positively because if we can't, who can we expect to? I have used positive affirmations a lot in my morning routine and general day to day life. I also tend to make a point of talking to myself positively before a race to prep me for the mileage I will cover by running, cycling or swimming. I always have a positive mantra when competing in sport and will say to myself in my mind with each step "I am strong, I am fit, I am healthy, I am powerful!" Try this the next time you're walking, cycling, running or swimming. I promise you will have a spring in your step. Twice a day at least I do this positive affirmation. I go through the entire alphabet and with each letter I say something positive, it always starts with the same phrase and you tag on the positive word at the end. "I am strong, I am fit, I am healthy, I am [insert Amazing, Brave, Courageous, Determined] but say each phrase all the way through for each letter of the alphabet. See what you come up with, it doesn't matter if you call yourself brave each time you get to 'B' it's just the positive message enforces to the subconscious.

Kindness Can Impact Your Heal

There are many beneficial effects in the body that kindness can be directly responsible for. Scientist David Hamilton is otherwise known as the Kindness Tsar and the Scottish doctor has written over 10 books on the subject.

If we think about stress on the body, the way that stress happens is through our thoughts. We feel a certain way and our body produces stress hormones like cortisol and adrenaline and before you know it we are experiencing a stress response. Our blood pressure rises and our cardiovascular system is put under pressure.

Kindness has the opposite effect. David Hamilton is a wonderful speaker and I encourage you to seek out some of his videos online on the science of kindness. He explains that when you are kind or see kindness happening for yourself, it creates a physiological response that is the opposite of stress.

Kindness is said to support the immune system. Research shows that when you are kind or see kindness in action, your immune system will boost an antibody known as secretory immunoglobulin A or s-IgA for short. This immune-boosting antibody is triggered not just by demonstrating kindness but witnessing it too. That's because kindness changes the way you feel and it is that feeling that promotes your body to boost the s-IgA antibody.

So you can experience this boost in s-IgA when you do nice things for others or help others but you can also experience the effect of s-IgA when you see a video of kindness in action, or you see someone demonstrate kindness in front of you. Maybe someone helps someone out, surprises someone with a gift or shows someone or an animal compassion (think about those dog rescue videos that get us all tearful!).

When the opposite happens, stress and the hormones of cortisol and adrenaline suppress immune function. Just like kindness, this doesn't have to be experiencing stress for yourself. You can stimulate these stress hormones just by watching something stressful. So that could be something you see online or watching something like a horror film. It could even be something like watching the news. When you expose yourself to too much of the world's negative news it can have a direct stressful impact on your immune response within your body. My advice? Go on a news fast!

If you want to increase your kindness boosting immunity, watch and share video clips and content that clearly demonstrates random acts of kindness, compassion and love. I always believe that you should follow social media accounts that uplift and inspire you. It's good for your mental health and it's great for your physiological health too.

Compassion is a feeling that is linked to kindness and usually triggers a kind act. Did you know that compassion and being kind can have an anti-inflammatory response? Actively practising kindness and compassion reduces inflammation by stimulating the vagus nerve. Both compassion and the inflammatory reflex is controlled in the vagus nerve so you could directly control the amount of inflammation in the body by being kind and compassionate.

Kindness also increases happiness and is said to be a good protector against feeling low and depression. Kindness can also change the brain structure thanks to neuroplasticity. Once upon a time, it was believed that our brains formed when we were young and that was that. We now know that the brain can experience neuroplasticity and change as we 'feed' our brains in a way that positively impacts its functional structure. In the same way, if you go to the gym and work your biceps your muscles in your arms will strengthen and grow, the same happens in your brain when you actively practise kindness on a regular basis. Brain scans have demonstrated that physical changes happen in the prefrontal cortex of the brain, biased to the left-hand side of the brain. This is the part of your brain that is behind and above your eyes and is known to be the area of the brain associated with positive emotion.

When you actively practise kindness and compassion, this frontal area grows and strengthens. Over time and with consistent kindness practice and witnessing kindness and compassion in action, this area becomes easier to access making positive emotions easier to access in this part of your brain. So you can actually use kindness to be happier and more positive!

Kindness to yourself and others strengthens a place within you that boosts self-worth, self-love and self-compassion. You get a great feeling within you if you are kind to others (and don't expect anything in return) and it can act as a proactive mechanism against depression.

Kindness in Business

There is lots of competition in business - healthy and unhealthy. I personally believe that there is enough business to go round and I don't like to live in a lack mentality. That is why I created my Ignite Your Creativity course to pass on my knowledge and experience to other people like I was on the start of my business journey. Yes, these people who do my course could potentially become my competition, but I do believe that there is enough for us all so I have always been happy to play mentor and teacher and save people the stresses and strains I experienced in setting up my business in the beginning.

As my business is me, my name on the tin (and the candle glass) then I am in the business to be kind because it is who I am as a person, but it is also my reputation in business at stake. I am responsible and I cannot hide behind a brand name or a business partner. My business is me and it is my responsibility.

I believe in being kind and patient and always delivering the most exceptional customer service. Whether I am working with a luxury hotel and creating bespoke private label candles or teaching someone how to create their own candle business from their kitchen table, you need to be kind. My favourite poem is If, by Rudyard Kipling. It is one of the most powerful pieces of writing that has always moved me and I have always drawn inspiration from. There is a line in the poem about being able to speak to all people at all levels, it states *'If you can talk with crowds and keep your virtue, or walk with Kings - nor lose the common touch'* and I think kindness is the key to this. It doesn't matter how successful you are, how rich you are, how powerful you are, you must always be kind. There is another wonderful quote which says:

'People will forget what you did, people will forget what you said, but people will never forget the way you made them feel.'

That's why focusing on exceptional customer service is the lifeblood for every small business. Little kind touches go a long way. I like to add personal handwritten notes to my orders. Yes, it takes a little bit of time but I genuinely love doing it and I know that my customers appreciate the small act of kindness. I will gift customers additional goodies and I will help with random acts of kindness where I can.

It is the acts of kindness that I do in private that bring me the most joy. I have sent items, books and literature that has changed my life to people I don't even know. That feeling that comes with knowing I have done something positive and possibly raised a smile in someone else makes me feel amazing and it is part of who I am. You might not be a person who finds giving gifts something that comes naturally. Your compliments, gratitude and words can go a long way to make someone feel appreciated and don't take much time or energy.

Always appreciate your customers and yes, they are always right. Even if they're difficult and complaining you can still deal with people with kindness. Remember I talked about that order of my glass candle votives that took over a year and 16% of my stock was lost? Even though I was really upset about the whole process, I made sure I was kind in all my dealings with the company. I know that upset and anger will not help the situation and will only make me feel negative and change my energy and state along with possibly upsetting someone else.

Always appreciate your staff and team members and remind them with words of affirmation of how their hard work has not gone unnoticed. People generally respond well to positive reinforcement and praise over punishment.

Be Kind to The Environment

I wanted to add this in because it is a huge passion of mine. I am so committed to environmental issues and climate change. I made a lot of changes in my business regarding the environment over the last couple of years and have been shortlisted in awards for my commitment to sustainable and ecologically friendly business. Sometimes my commitment to eco-friendly options does increase my bottom line and comes at a cost but I have found that my dedication to being as environmentally friendly as possible as a business has earned me respect from my customers, my community and wider business circles that I am a part of. Deciding to go plastic-free or announcing that I would be delivering my goods in boxes and packages that I would be reusing was a risk but it was one that paid off. I know I am doing my bit to help the local and wider environment and I hope to inspire other small businesses to follow suit. After all, they say that kindness is infectious so if we can all be kinder together in all ways, the world will be a happier and healthier place.

I always bless my food these days. It isn't a religious thing for me, it is an energy thing. I like to bestow loving, kind and grateful words over what I am about to eat as I feel it is important. I chose to go vegetarian after reading BOSH by Henry Firth and Ian Theasby and doing some research into energy and the effects on animals. I'd come across a video explaining that animals are flooded with stress hormones in the moment they know they are to be slaughtered. Apologies if you're not a vegetarian but I know my own views on energy and I didn't like the thought of eating the terrified energy of a living creature, so that was my turning point to go vegetarian. I am gradually trying to transition to a vegan lifestyle. This is no judgement on the food choices of anyone else, I just wanted to live in alignment with my beliefs, my love of animals and my beliefs on energy and quantum physics made this decision on my diet for me. My husband still eats fish but it's a veggie zone for my son and me.

Exercise: Being Kind

1. Where are you being unnecessarily unkind to yourself?
2. How can you reframe that unkindness into self-compassion? How can you be kinder? Write a loving and kind letter to yourself reminding yourself of all your amazing qualities.
3. What positive affirmations could you repeat to yourself every day?

Chapter 9

Master the Work/Life Challenge

"Never get so busy making a living that you forget to make a life."

-    Dolly Parton

When you're embarking on your entrepreneurial journey, and you have made that decision that you will go all in and set up your own business, it is exciting. Your whole life has the potential to change as you start and grow your business, and you know that it is going to take sheer determination, courage and time. Starting your own venture for the first time is terrifying, anxious, exhilarating and like stepping into the unknown. There are going to be so many things you will need to learn and adapt to, and it all takes time. Often, it is easy for your business to consume your every waking hour. There have been times on my own business journey when I have felt that all I do is work and sleep, but that is sometimes part and parcel of being an entrepreneur. It is how you deal with it and learn from it that makes the difference.

Often people will talk about a 'work/life balance', but I don't see things as balanced as that indicates that things are not moving, which they always are in both life and work. Every day is different, and one day I might work really late into the night, and the next day there is more family time and downtime. Being your own boss means you are often in charge of your own diary and time. If you have come away from a traditional 9-5 career and now find yourself at the mercy of your diary and plans it can be difficult to adjust. When you have been expected to follow the routines and working patterns of the traditional working world, your employer and your team, to suddenly be in charge of your day can leave you feeling a bit lost. Without the routine, accountability, processes and camaraderie of your team, you can find yourself wasting your day in a cycle of feeling like you don't know enough and don't know where to start. When you're a business owner, your daily routines are constantly changing and cyclic but being able to stick to as close as a routine as you can will really help you master the work/life challenge.

Where Do You Waste Time?

Ultimately, getting a work/life challenge in check comes down to time management. How you choose to spend your time will be the reason you feel like life is ticking along nicely, and you are in control or feeling completely swamped, burned out and overwhelmed.

I talk about this a lot with my friends who are also in business. When you love your business and love the feeling of running and growing your business, there are sacrifices to be made. One of the biggest sacrifices you can make when becoming an entrepreneur is to sacrifice wasting time on pastimes that the general population enjoy.

I'm really sorry for what I am about to say here, but soap operas are one such thing I would really get you to reconsider if these are one of your favourite pastimes. I often talk about when you are old in your chair and speaking to your grandkids, what will you tell them? All about your travel and your adventures? The money you made and places your success enabled you to go? The business lessons you learned and how you got to live a full and rich life? Or will you sit there and explain the ins and outs of watching a fake TV show about the exaggerated lives of others for decades? It just makes no sense to me. If you want to be in business, you have to be prepared to do the things that most people don't want to do. You have to sacrifice what is the 'norm' and what others feel like is part and parcel of modern culture. When you're retired, and you're on your boat in the ocean, reflecting on your life under the stars you won't be giving two hoots about Coronation Street or Eastenders.

Social media falls under this category too. I have to be honest and admit that I have struggled recently to curb my social media use. We are currently still in the middle of lockdown as I write this book during what I am sure you will all know as the COVID-19 pandemic. With a lack of routine and my business effectively closed, I have 'pivoted' and taken my skills and knowledge online to sell my online courses. This means that all of my marketing is now online, and as such, I spend more time on social media. It is too easy to waste time on these platforms, and I have had to introduce strict measures to reduce my time scrolling. This requires discipline and determination, but I know it is important if I am to continue to write my book, grow my business and prepare for life post-pandemic.

We all need to reclaim our time if we want to live our lives to the fullest in our personal and business lives. Let's look at what is important to you and how you will choose to spend that time.

Work Out What is Important to You

In Chapter 5, Your Ideal Day I got you to think about the rocks, pebbles and sand in your life. You might need to revisit this exercise for this chapter too. What did you write for your rocks? Your pebbles and your sand? This is the time to think about fitting in all of those things into your life.

You will always have time to fit into your life what is important to you. It is just how we work! If you decide that it is important for you to scroll on social media for hours, guess what? You will fit that time in. If you decide that it is important for you to work out first thing in the morning, guess what? You will fit that time in for your workout. You will make the time. If you suddenly decide that you will prioritise getting enough sleep at night, guess what? You'll find yourself stopping that next episode of that TV show or stop scrolling on your phone in bed. You make time for the things that are important to you. We each get the same amount of time each day, but it is what you do with it and how you fill your time that counts.

Next time you find yourself using the excuse "I haven't got time" please re-frame it immediately with "That isn't important to me right now." Because the way you feel in that moment after speaking that sentence will determine whether you can make the time for whatever it is you're not committing to. This works both ways. If you say "I haven't got time to go and see my mum/sister/grandad" what you're really saying is "It is not important to me right now to see my mum/sister/grandad" and actually that might be the truth and might be perfectly acceptable. Yet if you keep telling yourself that you want to see more of your relatives, but you keep putting it off, this sentence might make you realise that you do need to carve out some time for a visit. If you say to yourself that you really want to lose weight but you "haven't got time to go to the gym" then using this tip here, what you're really saying is "Losing weight isn't important to me." If it IS important to you, then you must do what thousands of other successful people have done to lose weight and make the time to train, plan your healthy meals and track your food or follow whatever plan works for you.

Fitting It All In

I don't want to write this book and make you feel like you all of a sudden have to become a 5 am get up queen, triathlete and successful business owner in one. I understand the pressures of having a family, responsibilities, personal goals and a business. Fitting it all in sometimes feels like an impossible juggling task. Here are some examples of wanting to do more in less time and the decisions you may have to make;

Yes, you want to run in the morning, but you also want to stay up late watching TV with your partner. Trying to do both will leave you depleted and exhausted as your sleep duration suffers. You have to decide which one you want more.

Yes, you want to learn that language, but you also want to scroll for hours on social media catching up what everyone has been up to. Trying to do both will leave you frazzled and overwhelmed. We only have a limited amount of time each day. You have to decide which one means more to you.

Yes, you want to set up your own business, but you are also working in your full-time job. Trying to do both is possible, but you might need to make a decision to sacrifice other things in your life or invest in ways to work smarter to help you reach your goal quicker.

What do you want more? Whenever you want to master the work/life challenge, ask yourself what is most important to you. What means the most? Is there something you can work on and dedicate time to that will have an overall positive knock-on effect on other goals you want to achieve?

Running with Determination

Around six years ago, I decided to start running. It isn't something I had ever really taken seriously, and I did feel completely out of my depth. I always say that the hardest part was lacing up my trainers and getting out of the door on the day of that first session. My friend was supposed to come too but couldn't make it, so I just decided to go for it, which was further reflected in all my subsequent events. You have to have the strength to go it alone; otherwise, you'll still be in the same spot. It can be daunting going to a group for the first time, but boldness has power. I was terrified going along to my Allsorts running group (named because there are all sorts of us with all sorts of different abilities) yet it turned out to be the most fantastic journey I've ever been on. It is a supportive, loving, fun and crazy motivational group, and I am proud to be an Allsort.

I didn't get great at running after that one session. It has taken years of consistent practice and effort. It got easier each time. I got expert help in the form of the coaches, my fellow run club members supported me, and I set myself goals. It gave me a taste for determination and self-discipline. I followed my training plan and felt pride as my times improved and my body responded to the training with more strength and stamina.

The process of training for a goal isn't about the medal and adulation at the end. It is about proving to yourself that you can keep your promises. It is one thing that people say about me "You always do what you say you will do." I am not a special person; I don't possess more willpower than most. I have just become completely addicted to that feeling of elation when you see things through until the end.

In the last six years, I have run marathons in the UK and New York. I completed a 100 mile Olympic Challenge, and in 2017 I ran the equivalent length of Britain. I ran over 1000 miles in a year. If I make a decision that I am doing something, I don't delay it to some point in the future; I start it as soon as possible. Not prone to making New Year's resolutions, the challenge of running 1000 miles in a year came completely out of the blue.

I knew I could physically run the miles if I stayed injury-free; it was the mind game that would be the hardest to master. That craving and need for us to keep warm, comfortable and in our safe zones is sometimes the most dangerous place to be. A life without purpose and too comfortable has never been the path for me, and I was lucky that my running buddy Lynne is as resilient and mentally focused as me. Lynne and I worked out that in order to clock the 1000 miles needed for the challenge, we would have to run around 2.73 miles a day or just over 19 miles a week. We aimed for a marathon a week, 26 miles, to allow for any potential spots of injury or illness. We had a few other running challenges where we would 'absorb' the miles. We had signed up for the Edinburgh marathon, New York Marathon, a couple of half marathons, and a duathlon. We signed up initially with around 90 others and watched online as we all tracked our mileage each week. Even though I had responsibilities at home with my family and my business to run, I ensured I made the time to complete the distance. I'd carve out a few miles in the mornings or some in the evenings and try to do long training runs on a weekend while my family still slept.

What really shocked and surprised me about running a marathon a week for a year was how much of a mental fortitude challenge it turned out to be. It forced me to get even more organised and laser-focused in my life. I would plan runs around work and family time, school runs and social activities. I was so fuelled by determination and discipline that I was constantly thinking about the miles, and I do mean constantly. On one occasion we were going to a 25th wedding anniversary party about 12 miles away, and I ran there! The whole year was definitely a mind game.

According to James Clear, author of Atomic Habits, it takes anywhere from 2-8 months to develop a new behaviour or habit which is why so many of us struggle to maintain the momentum needed to really change. Coupled with the fact that according to Forbes, 80% of people give up their New Year's resolution by the second week in February, the odds were stacked against me. Yet I knew once I set my mind to it, I was doing it. At the start of the challenge, on January 1, 2017, I took a picture knowing I wanted to take one exactly a year later and witness the changes. When I took and then observed the picture taken a year later on January 1, 2018, I felt emotional at the image staring back at me. There was no great physical difference, but I could see the subtle differences in my posture, smile and determination behind my eyes. That challenge showed me exactly what I am capable of. That challenge allowed me to trust myself to follow through with my personal pledges and mileage. It started as a running race across a year, and it finished as a life-changing mindset shift within me that had the most positive knock-on effect in both my personal life and my business. I realised what I could achieve when I set my mind to it. I realised what I could get done with meticulous planning. It made me better in business for sure.

#100 Books in a Year

The next year I set myself another annual challenge. This time I decided to read 100 books in a year. Due to my lack of an academic start in my youth, there had never been an emphasis on my reading skills, and it was something I wanted to improve. Loving all things self-development, I asked people I admired for their similar energy and values and compiled a list of their recommended reads. I established a routine of reading in the mornings and evenings. Then during my working day, I would listen to audiobooks.

This challenge might not have been as physically demanding as running 1000 miles in a year, but it took up a lot of time and a lot of brain space. I was learning something new every single day. It broadened my knowledge and my thinking. I found I was participating in conversations in a much more rich and comprehensive manner. I challenged previous values and thought processes. I strengthened my resolve, and some of the books forced me to look deeper within myself than I had ever done before. Reading for hours every day became a delight. I soaked up everything I learned and began putting things into practice. I was constantly adding more into my life but always feeling like my new knowledge, habits, and skill gave me more quality time. I pretty much stopped watching TV and consuming media. I sadly lost a few friends around this time, too as my new open-minded and expansive thinking challenged the norm. I didn't want to meet to constantly belittle others, not present who were unable to stick up for themselves. I was stared at blankly and sometimes with annoyance for trying to share an alternative perspective - from the point of view of the person intended to be the victim for that particular bitching session. I realised some people were not for me anymore, we had grown apart, but that was OK. I was happy with my quest for growth, and if it meant losing a few friends who would keep my wings clipped, it was time to let go and fly that negative nest.

This also taught me a great lesson in my business too. There were some professional events, and networking opportunities that were not in my vibe, and the people were not my tribe. I often thought I needed to get out and constantly network in order to put my business out there.

I realised in reading these books that looking for outside validation and recognition of others was linked to my own self worth issues and lack of confidence in my business. The learning I did through those 100 books gave me so much wisdom, knowledge and food for thought. I started to put things into practice in my home life and my work life, and I gained confidence all round.

They say that a lack of confidence just comes back to a lack of knowledge. When you don't know something or how to do something you feel nervous and anxious, worried about making even a single step. As soon as you gain knowledge or experience, your confidence grows. I felt this shift in me, too, when reading all those books. They gave me the gift of knowledge, which in turn gave me the confidence I needed to grow my business and drop the need for validation from others.

#Swimming the Channel - Twice!

In late 2018 I decided my challenge would be to swim the length of the Channel. This is a charity event for Aspire supporting those with spinal cord injuries. Luckily it doesn't involve an actual Channel crossing; you are able to complete this anywhere in the world as long as you have access to a body of water. It involved swimming 22 miles in your own time, tracking the mileage and raising money for charity. I did this in my local swimming pool over 12 weeks, clocking up a minimum of 118 lengths a week to make the distance. I completed this quite easily. After running the equivalent of a marathon every week in the previous year, this challenge seemed like a walk in the park.

Which is why in typical Jo fashion, I couldn't help but completely turn it up a notch the next year. Now I never like doing the same race or challenge twice - you know you can do it, so why not try something different? But I really wanted to repeat this challenge as Aspire is a great cause. I knew I could completely eradicate my zone of comfort by repeating the challenge in 2019 but this time pledging to do it in the open water in the icy, temperamental Scottish sea by my home.

I started the outdoor swim challenge in September. Swimming in the open seas is absolutely terrifying in comparison to a pool. The temperatures, the tides, the darkness at points leave you disorientated. I got a book of tides and marked off the high tide times in my calendar. These would be my appointments to swim. In September I was swimming in the sea in just a bathing costume.

Pretty soon within a matter of weeks, I was fully rubber-suited in my wet suit and wondering what on earth I'd let myself in for?! The challenge was due to end in December. Still, by early October I knew that I either ramped up the mileage and swam more in the early days or ended up potentially in a state of hypothermia if it nudged towards the festive season and I still had miles left to go.

I chose the former and started to swim as much as possible. There was nothing quite like the feeling of that wall of biting cold, powerful water each time I entered the sea. Each time I wondered what the hell I was doing, but I did it anyway! It made me even more unwavering in my approach. There were times when the tides threatened to slam me into the rocks, and there were moments where I wondered if hypothermia had set in. There were also a couple of night swims that I did which were liberating and frightening in equal measure. Being guided by the moonlight and glimmer of light from the lamps on the shore made the experience all the more unusual. At times I was physically losing my sense of direction in those choppy unpredictable waters, yet in my mind, I was more focused on the direction of my life than ever before.

Having the courage to break through a personal plateau and put yourself in a vulnerable position of the unknown is truly life-changing. There is a wonderful phrase that states "How you do one thing is how you do everything." I know in my heart that setting myself these challenges and moving heaven and hell to get them completed has changed me as a person, and this leaks into so many other areas of my life. If I say I am doing something in my business, I do it! I used to freak out at an order for 60 candles and wonder how on earth I'd find the time. Now if an order for 600 candles comes in, I cope better than I ever have before. I take a look at my life and available time then logically assess whether I can do it. If so, I formulate a plan.

Mastering a Personal Challenge

During 2019 my husband went through a cancer battle that required extended periods of time in hospital. Soon our comfortable lives of family time, school, business, fun and my fitness challenges had hospital appointments and intensive periods of needing to care for my sick husband thrown into the mix. At this time I could've given in. I could've thrown in the towel on everything and let my emotions and fear take over. I think my experience with my challenges and the mental fortitude that has occurred since set me up well to cope with this challenging time. I wasn't numb or indifferent; I rallied round to care for my husband and also ensure our son's needs were met. I still ran my business at the same pace, and I still swam in the sea and ran around the park with Archie. I think on reflection; it was taking part in these activities and keeping my promises to myself that enabled me to cope with the unexpected cancer diagnosis and treatment. I didn't give up on myself at a time when it would've been easy to drop everything thinking I had to be at my husband's bedside in every spare moment. I feel like I did him a better service by continuing my challenges and therefore continuing to forge my mental toughness and resilience. I have never been more fearful or out of my comfort zone than at that time when my husband took ill, but it was getting out of my personal comfort zone on a daily basis that gave me the strength to support him in the best and strongest way possible.

I'm not writing this as a ploy to say "Look at me and all I have done and coped with." I am writing this firstly as a reminder to myself of all I am capable of. I am an ordinary woman in my forties who made a decision to be determined, and that determination has shaped every part of me to the core.

I believe that we are all capable of so much more than we all realise. I also believe that in order to be a success in business, you have to be a success in your personal life too. One should not take over the other; they can work in harmony and the things you do in your personal life can have a direct positive impact on the things you do in your business life and vice versa.

Other Quick Tips for Mastering the Work/Life Challenge

1. Turn off devices at the dinner table. Your work can wait. It was Jim Rohn who said; "When you are at work, be at work. When you are home, be at home". Emails and social media notifications will still be there 30 mins after you have eaten. There is a whole generation failing to read body language because most of their communication is on screen. Take your time with your food and use the dinner table as a time to connect and converse with your loved ones. My husband and son would much prefer to have a TV dinner, but I'm strict on this - dinner on the table in the dining room and a chance for real and loving connection. It is crucial we do not lose the art of communicating as a family, and this is one of my non-negotiable actions.

2. Assess what TV programmes are costing you. I know we all want to feel like we have common ground with people and I know everyone might be raving about that latest show on Twitter or sending memes about the characters on

Whatsapp. Do you have hours to invest in a TV show if you're setting up a business? Netflix and Prime Video want to keep you watching for longer. Series that could be made in 3 episodes are dragged out to 10. Can you afford to spend 10 hours on a TV programme you might not even like? Or would those 10 hours be better spent working on your business?

3. Have boundaries in your business hours. Don't feel the need to answer Facebook messages to your business page or emails after 5 pm and over the weekends. I know this might not be possible in every business and every sector but don't be scared to have set hours and boundaries for yourself and your customers. Create an auto-response on your email and your social media inboxes that tells customers when you respond and the times you are available.

4. Have a morning routine for your life and one for your business. This does not need to take a long time at all but knowing what you have coming up that day and a general idea of how long things will take you will help you manage your time more effectively.

5. "Pay yourself first" - in all aspects of your life. Put money away first when you get paid, and you will survive on the money left. If you put your money away when you get paid, it is done and taken care of. This is the same principle for exercise. Exercise first, and you will get it done. Leave it until later in the day, and it becomes so much harder. Starting earlier puts you in a positive mindset and makes you feel like you have achieved something. This also applies

for your big red flag jobs; the eat that frog job that is difficult. Get it done first, and it is out of the way! If you struggle with any of these things, I highly recommend getting some form of accountability in terms of an exercise buddy, mentor or coach.

6.   Plan the important stuff in your life first—family, health, work and fun. Remember the exercise on rocks, pebbles and sand. Get those really important things in your diary and STICK TO THEM. This is vital.

7.   Have things to look forward to. Make weekend plans with your family. Organise things and don't wait for others if you want stuff to happen. The simplest of things help keep our family connected; walks in nature, quality time together or fun activities that you all enjoy. Book onto business events that will strengthen your knowledge and networks (if appropriate) and give you some well-needed breaks from your day to day business routines.

8.   Make sure you leave some time in your day for nothing. For when the plans go a bit awry, or you just want a space to be and think and create. Remember it is like a glass of water, and if that glass is full, there is no room for any more water.

Exercise: Master the Work/Life Challenge

1.   Where are you saying you don't have time for things that are actually really important to you?
2.   What could you do in your life to help have work/life brilliance? (*Balance would ordinarily fit here but, I believe*

balance indicates stillness and being stationary so I like to have a flow and call it work/life brilliance instead).

3. Are there any challenges you would love to attempt that would help you see what you are capable of? *(Bonus points if you sign up for one right after reading this chapter!)*

Chapter 10

Pack Your Entrepreneur Toolbag

"Build a firm foundation with the bricks others have thrown at you."
- David Brinkley

When you start in business and even as you move along your entrepreneurial journey, you are going to naturally pick up different tools to help you at different stages of your business growth and with business tasks.

Some tools may land in your lap or cross over from previous employment. New tools may get recommended by fellow business owners, mentors, coaches or like-minded contacts in online groups. I know that a lot of the tools in my own entrepreneur toolbag have been tried and tested, sharpened and polished over the years. Some tools I really wish I'd had at the start of my own business journey so I wanted to share some of them with you that I hope will inspire you, assist you in your business and save you precious time and resources.

Business Tools

Technology Tools

Notifications are a teensy weensy bugbear of mine. Apparently it takes around 40 minutes to get into your 'flow zone' and then for every time you get distracted, it takes on average 23 minutes to get those creative juices flowing again. One of the ways you can certainly disrupt your flow is by having your notifications on across all your devices. You can be in the middle of something juicy and important and then off go your notifications - Ping! Ping! Ping! Then 'ping' goes your schedule down the drain for the day.

I made the conscious decision to turn all my notifications off a couple of years ago. I could see the time and energy that they were taking up and how they were stopping me from performing at my best in my work. Turning off notifications means I am very much in charge of my own time and someone else isn't dictating the flow of my day and 'to-do list'. I only have myself to blame for procrastinating.

Now that I have no notifications to disturb me, including my emails being off and my phone out of reach, I get into that amazing 'flow state' otherwise known as 'being in the zone'. You'll know this feeling - time feels like it stops still and you are so immersed in your task at hand that you feel totally at peace, calm and fully involved in something you love. Your productivity goes through the roof.

When I first did this, it felt alien and quite hard. I worried what people would think if I didn't get back to them right away. Soon I could see the benefits as my output seemed to double, and work felt more relaxed and more enjoyable. These days I think it is completely normal to work distraction-free. I highly recommend it. In fact, I'm going to be a bit bossy. If you want to really rocket your productivity, then be brave and turn off your notifications. Go on, turn them off now, I'm waiting....

Yes, in case you were wondering, I do have the ringer on so I do ask people to ring me if it is urgent. At one point, I was given an Apple Watch. I thought this was brilliant at first! Until I realised that it tapped me on the wrist like I was a naughty child if I didn't stand up every hour. It drove me mad, so I gave it to my son.

If you do struggle with distractions from notifications or social media alerts, then there are many plugins or apps that you can get for your computer or devices that can restrict access to certain websites or social media apps. Depending on whether you use a Mac or PC, there are different options. Just do a Google search for 'distraction apps', and you'll find plenty on the market that can help you to stay on your tasks in hand.

Software and Apps for your Toolbag

Mailchimp - When you build a business and nurture your audience, one of the best forms of marketing is an email list. Building your email list should be done from the get-go. Email is much more direct and intimate and helps build relationships between you and your customers. Mailchimp is where I keep my email database of customers. It is hooked up to Facebook and my sign up form on my website to capture contacts that want to be informed first of what is happening. I send those on my email list my special offers and events before anyone else. I also send out a monthly newsletter to keep a line of communication with my customers past and present. You can track opens and connect it to your shop too and can track sales that come in as a result of that particular newsletter that went out.

Survey monkey – A great tool for gathering market research, I have just launched my first survey to gather information for my first Advanced Candle Making Workshop. You can make your surveys anonymous which means you will get real and honest feedback. This is great for refining your products and services. Being able to take the criticism is key and not take it to heart. The negative feedback can be as useful as the positive as it allows you to tweak your products and services to make them even better.

Google Analytics - View your website traffic and where it's coming from and monitor your conversion rates, see your demographics and which device your customers use. When you know this data, you'll know how best to communicate with your audience. It seems complex, but Google Analytics is a valuable tool for every online business.

Social Media

If you're going to be on social media and you're going to do it well, the clue is in the title - be *social*.

I love social media, and I love being social. I hosted Twitter hour @Elevenseshour for about a year, just a casual networking hour to see if I could help a fellow small business out. We would chat about coffee and cake and make fabulous connections. It amazes me that some people would come on with the hard sell; "Look what I'm selling today" - almost like an interruption in the flow of the conversation. You wouldn't do that if you were all standing around drinking coffee or at the water cooler now would you? So get involved in discussions, show you care about people, take an interest and be kind. There is a lot of negativity on social media (particularly Twitter), and it is good practice to be kind. You don't have to be negative or moan about people or events on Twitter for all to see.

People totally forget that there is usually someone behind the social media account, there are some bots out there and auto DMs which have their place, but the world and business are all about people.

We all want followers, don't we? We always compare ourselves to others and wonder why the last person unfollowed you doing their 'follow unfollow' strategy. If you haven't heard of this, it is where someone will spend time following a number of accounts. It is natural for people to feel obliged to follow back, and they do. The original person who followed you will then go back and unfollow the accounts they just followed. It is done a lot, but for me, it feels like an unethical and strange tactic to try and gather followers.

The topic of followers is something I am passionate about. Do not measure your worth against the number of followers you have. A sure-fire way to make yourself feel rubbish is to compare yourself to anything. It is better to build fans than collect fair-weather followers. You can have a million followers, but if they aren't engaged in you, your product or service, you won't necessarily have a million customers. Likes are not a direct reflection of profits, and it's better to have 100 highly engaged followers who love what you do and buy from you regularly than 10,000 passive followers who don't know who you are and couldn't care less about you.

Never never ever buy followers, however tempting it might be. It may look good for a second, but they are not in your market. They are not your customers, and that is one of the main reasons you will put your time, energy and effort into your social media. Want to know how to spot someone who has bought followers? Look at their engagement rates every time they post something. How many people like and comment on the posts? Is this relative to the number of followers they have? If someone has 80K followers and they post something or tweet and get 13 likes, there is something wrong. You just have to look at the engagement rate of anything they post subsequently and see how low it is to spot bought followers. It doesn't help you at all, and you will have to keep ploughing money at your social profiles to grow them that way. Then you may be tempted to not make much of an effort on your account as it looks like you have all the followers you need - albeit unengaged ones.

I love using social media to connect other people. Nothing makes me happier than to connect two people or businesses that can potentially help each other. I don't follow up afterwards to ask if they emailed or sent one another a follow-up message. I have made the connection, and it is up to the person to act. Some people never do, and you think that was on a plate for you there and you didn't do anything about it! So if you're offered as a recommendation from someone - follow up! It is so hard selling yourself sometimes, and word of mouth marketing and recommendations from others goes a long way. All you need to do is send a message and connect, and who knows? A new client, customer or large scale order for your product or service could land in your lap.

Having said I love social media, there has to be a place for it. Is there anyone else incredibly concerned by people out in social groups all on their phones. I saw a family recently in a restaurant. There were six of them from toddler age up to late 60s, and ALL of them were staring into their own screens, none of them connecting with any other person. It went on for pretty much the whole meal and made me so sad to witness it. I see Frankie and Benny's have banned screens in their UK restaurants to attempt to connect people over food again. I think this is a fantastic idea although I don't think we need an establishment to do that we should be making these decisions ourselves. Apparently a generation are failing to recognise body language, voice tone and facial features because of their increasing interaction with screens. This is all very worrying, considering that most of our communication is non-verbal.

When you are on social media, keep it real and never be someone who you are not. There is a chance or two that you might eventually meet a real live person from social media, who follows you. As my son always says in his funny tone "It's IRL, mum!" (meaning "in real life"). Make sure your online persona fits that of your real true self. There would be nothing more embarrassing than meeting someone who has this outrageous flamboyant online presence to only discover they are a shy and hermit type person. Also, people see through fakeness in social media. They can tell in your eyes and your body language whether you're pretending to be something you're not. Make sure your biography across your social media presence and your website is true to self too. If you were reading about someone who loves cross stitch, baking for the church sale and collecting stamps, then you build a picture up about them and know they will be different from the person who likes extreme sports, brewing their own beer and camping. Make it easier for people to work with you by giving your true persona. People buy people! It's an old cliche, but it is so true.

Social Media Tools I Swear By

Twitter – This has probably had the biggest impact of all my social media channels. It's very much business to business, and you can use it without getting involved in the negative news-driven drama that happens on the platform each day. Make sure you get a name that syncs with your brand and portrays the image of your business or personal style. It amazes me how many people still have an 'egg avatar' as their profile picture. I personally don't connect with anyone who still has an egg. If there is anything you are going to do first, make it that.

In 2015, I got involved in Theo Paphitis' small business social media initiative called Small Business Sunday. To get involved, you tweet him on a Sunday afternoon in a two-hour window and tweet about your business. At the time, Twitter's character count was only 140 characters per tweet, so you had to be clever and concise in explaining to the retail giant what your business did and how it helped people. I did this religiously every Sunday for over a year. I tweeted different tweets to Theo Paphitis every week, and on Monday morning I would eagerly log into Twitter hoping to have been chosen as one of only six businesses that would be showcased by Theo that week. I did this every week, I never lost faith, I realised it only took five minutes out of my Sundays and actually it was really nice to put into words exactly what I did, and why I was proud of my business. After over a year of doing this, one Monday morning I grabbed my phone to check and open Twitter and could see the notifications had gone a bit crazy. I had been picked! It felt amazing. I was featured on the front page of his website and given the opportunity as a Small Business Sunday winner to get invited to Theo Paphitis networking and business events.

Every year he has a huge event in Birmingham that he brings business owners along to. You can get interviews with his sub-companies like Boux Avenue, Rymans and Robert Dyer so if you had a product that could be in these shops, you could have a free 15-minute meeting with the buyers. I went to this event in Birmingham once and it was amazing. Us business owners would get to see great speakers and leaders in the business field including Mike Pickles from the Really Useful Boxes company and Holly Tucker from Not On The High Street.

Winning Small Business Sunday that week gave me the boost and confidence to find more opportunities via Twitter for small businesses like mine. I was a winner of Jacqueline Gold's Women on Wednesday feature and I also applied to take part in a Shop Local Shop Small campaign hosted by an organisation called Small Business Saturday.

Pretty much like my communication with Theo Paphitis and Jacqueline Gold, I would get involved in the @smallbizsaturday Twitter conversations. The Small Business Saturday campaign also has an additional feature whereby 100 businesses are chosen from thousands that apply to be featured in a special 100-day campaign called The Small Business 100. This campaign gets great coverage in the media and online and 100 businesses each are given a day to showcase their products or services in the run-up to the first Saturday in December. It is run at this time to act as the antithesis to Black Friday. In 2017 I applied for one of the prestigious 100 places and was successful! As one of the 100 businesses chosen for the campaign I had my own assigned day where I was featured in the local media and across many social media platforms.

Small Business Saturday as a whole gets some great press coverage nationally and internationally. I was mentioned in an article in Forbes which was such a personal and business highlight for me. Along with featuring the businesses, the campaign has many in-person events including a special Small Business Saturday bus that tours the UK visiting different cities. The bus houses the Small Business Saturday team and offers mentoring sessions and Q&A sessions live from the Small Business Couch. It is such a brilliant initiative and so important for small businesses across the UK. They estimate that 99% of all UK businesses are classed in the category of 'small business' so without us small businesses we would have no economy! That is why it is so important to support local - even if it is just through raising awareness on social media. Participating in Small Business Saturday and being chosen as one of 100 businesses across the UK was so good for my business - raising awareness of me, my candles and my courses. It also acted as a wonderful PR opportunity earning me local and national press coverage which further celebrated my business, improved my reputation and gave me great 'social proof' in the media.

In 2017, being chosen as one of the 100 businesses I was over the moon to be invited to a drinks reception at Downing Street - home of the UK Prime Minister. As I left my hotel, I jumped in a taxi armed with a box full of my candles which was a hoot. "Where ya goin' there, lahv?" said the cockney Hackney driver as I got in. "10 Downing Street please!" I said with a chuckle. He definitely thought I was joking. "No really, I have been invited to 10 Downing Street." he turned around and looked at me as if to say "You stayed in a Hub by Premier Inn last night and now you want to go to Downing Street?" it was hilarious.

It was stunning inside and very homely, I swanned up and down the stairs a few times, all the faces of past Prime Ministers watching. The artworks were beautiful and of course real paintings - not a print in sight. I even spotted a piece of moon rock encased in acrylic gifted by President Nixon.

As part of the event, 20 product-based businesses were invited to have a table displaying what our business offered and a chance to showcase our stock. I was shocked and excited to be announced as one of those 20 businesses and the photo of me showcasing my candles in Downing Street is an image I treasure. Displaying my products was not to try and get sales, but the prestige of being inside Number 10 Downing Street was more than enough and the networking was incredible. I chatted with Baroness Fairhead and Stephen Barclay. I did make 100 special limited edition Jo Macfarlane Small Business Saturday Christmas candles that were given to all the final businesses from across the country and presented to everyone at the event. It was my way of giving back to all the businesses that had been chosen as the 100 from across the UK and celebrating small business.

In 2018 I was invited to Number 11 Downing Street to a drinks reception with the Chancellor of the Exchequer and Small Business Saturday alongside 50 other businesses. This was another wonderful experience and chance to mingle with fellow small business owners and make fabulous connections. I still pinch myself that this happened for me. It gave me so much press coverage, and it elevated my status. All because I answered a call out on Twitter and got involved in business conversations on the social media platform. Twitter is worth using when it is used right, I promise.

Linkedin - As you will probably already be aware, LinkedIn is a more business-oriented social networking platform designed for professionals. It is a place to connect with people in your niche, and if you are looking to connect with an editor of a magazine or publication to get PR coverage, I will connect here. Prior to an event I would also connect with the guest list if that was public. It is also a good tool for follow-ups after an event too.

Facebook – It's a great tool but businesses beware that if you are running your business from a Facebook page the customers belong to Facebook. If it was to go down tomorrow, your customers would go with it. Your posts are not always shown to everyone too. If you want to make sure that you control what your customers are seeing, then it is best to own your website or at least email database. Combine Facebook with The Social Sales Girls who teach Facebook ads and how to target your customers.

YouTube - needs no explanation, but video is the way forward and drives more engagement. This is the second biggest search engine in the world. I like to repurpose my social media videos and add them to YouTube too. Think of it as yet another online advertisement board. Don't neglect it as replicating content to YouTube is worth the time and effort. Once you have placed your video, you can turn it into an ad through Google ads and target your demographic audience. Use Rev.com to put subtitles on your video.

Buffer – Is a social media scheduling tool with analytics. You can look back on your most popular posts, tweets, and schedule the next month or week ahead. Posting organically works well, but it's great to write and schedule a chunk of content in advance. I love the feeling that messages are going out while I am working on something else. It gives me peace of mind that my social media marketing is still happening without me having to post everything 'as live'. It also has a 'content' stream so you can add accounts that your customers would be engaged in, pick and choose what you think they would like to read and add it to your schedule. Important note: Always always always read any article to the end or watch a video to the end before you share it with your audience. It could contain views that may not align with your brand values. You just never know what might pop up at the end.

Photography Apps

Whether you are a product-based business or you offer a service, and your business brand is you, you will always need good quality photography to help make your social media and marketing 'pop' and stand out.

While I am not a photographer, I have taken many courses and followed business photography professionals who are always giving hints and advice. Here are some of the best photography apps and advice I use in my business.

Dropbox - allows you to share large photos and files onto the cloud. It syncs with my phone too so always saves all of my photo images. This is great peace of mind knowing my images are safe - even if I were to break or lose my phone.

iMovie - Video editing software. I recommend that you get a lapel microphone, iPhone stand and ring light. This will really make your videos stand out. Remember - you have around 3 seconds to make an impact on a video, so investing in some inexpensive technology will help make your videos stand out.

Vimeo - For converting videos into MP4 which is compatible with my website. You can keep the video private, share links or make it public. You can also embed videos into your email marketing using either Vimeo or YouTube.

Pinterest – A visual adult scrapbooking social media site. I love Pinterest! It is a fabulous place to draw inspiration for business projects and also for personal design inspiration for your home. As I am a very visual person I love Pinterest and use it a lot. In the workbook I will show you how to grow your Pinterest from 0 - 220,000 visits in a few simple steps. I would also highly recommend running ads on Pinterest to your target audience to drive sales or engagement in your online platforms.

Asana – A great app to keep all your tasks and projects in one place. This is a brilliant tool to stay productive and on track with all your projects. There is nothing quite like writing with pen and paper, and I love that, however, there is a lot to be said for keeping a master list all in one place.

Snapseed - a super little app on the phone for modifying pictures. You can edit a photo to look very professional using one of the many filters available.

Wordswag - Great app for stock images and social media posts. You can add wording over your posts from your phone and get them posted in minutes.

Canva - A valuable drag and drop graphic design tool for creating across the board consistency with your branding. You can create social media posts, postcards, presentations, posters and even t-shirts!

You can download the designs ready to post onto social media or get things printed directly from the app to be delivered to your business. Be aware that Canva printing prices can be on the expensive side.

Lightroom - I wouldn't put a picture out on social media until it had been through Lightroom, a photo editing tool. This is done via the desktop rather than a mobile device. There are many Lightroom presets that you can purchase. These can be overlayed onto your images to deliver a consistency with exposure, composition and colours of your images. It can take a little while to get to grips with the editing on Lightroom, but Adobe has plenty of tutorial videos.

Vistaprint - For flyers and printed material, Vistaprint is a great all-rounder. If you need well-produced quality printed goods then you can't go wrong here.

Moo - For something a bit more quirky including miniature business cards then Moo is also another good printing company. Limited to stickers, business cards, postcards and notebooks but really good branding, designs, paper quality and quick delivery.

Toolbag for the Readers
As you will have probably gathered reading this book, I am a huge fan of lifelong learning and reading. Here are some of my favourite reading apps and tools that can help you keep on track with your reads, listen to audiobooks and find other places which act as a learning resource.

Mad Reader - If you are a crazy reader like me this is a great way of keeping track of the books you have read. Just scan the QR code to add it. I have read a few books twice before I had this, but then I think I was supposed to read some of those books twice!

Audible - At the time of writing, the monthly subscription fee for Audible is £7.99 a month which gives you one credit for one book a month. Or you can get a boost and pay £18 for three books a month. Watch out for free books and special deals that crop up.

Podcasts - Always great to listen to an inspirational talk. You can listen to podcasts through many streaming services including the Podcasts app on Apple Devices, Spotify, RadioPublic, Pocket Casts, Castbox, Podbean, Overcast, ListenApp and Stitcher.

iTunes - Create a playlist for yourself that inspires and excites you, create a chill playlist too. I love having playlists already made and have music to hand that I can play whatever I'm trying to get done, or whatever state I'd like to be in. Music has the power to instantly change my energy.

Banking Toolbag

Go Henry - This is an app for finances and children. You are given a visa debit card that is attached to the Go Henry app. As a parent you can set spend limits on the card but you can also top up the funds instantly from the app. Great for asking relatives to send birthday and Christmas money too as they can pay directly into the Go Henry account via a shareable link. I love how this also manages my son's pocket money and keeps him on top of his tasks. If he doesn't do his chores, he doesn't get his pocket money!

Moneybox - This clever financial app rounds up all your purchases to the nearest pound and can save the difference into an ISA account or into ISA stocks and shares. As with any apps around investing, please do your own research into the investments which carry an element of risk.

Chip & Plum - Both are automatic savings accounts. Chip uses a separate app while Plum integrates with Facebook messenger. Every time you get a deposit into your bank account - for example your wages, the software will make an automatic saving for you. This is a great way to build savings without even noticing.

Hiring Help

When you start your own business you wear many hats and feel like you do absolutely everything. This is completely normal on the entrepreneur journey and I'd argue it is a process that you have to go through. There may be some elements of your business that you're actually quite good at but would never have known. Maybe you're a graphic design ninja, or a marketing wizard. Maybe you're brilliant at sales. For those tasks that drag and have you stressed out and needing to delegate, always be brave and outsource if you're in a financial position to. You will be amazed at how much energy you free up to create more abundance in your business.

Moneypenny - Virtual PA for messaging and calls. From hosting live chats to a fully functioning telephone answering service. This gives you a business phone number for around £20 a month. It adds an air of professionalism and protects my time too as they field the queries and calls that come in. You can also set it up so that a caller will press a relevant number to speak to you about different matters. For example "Press 1 to book a workshop, 2 to speak to someone about private label candles, 3 for accounts" etc. If you don't want to field a query from any of these you can set it so that you are not available to answer and the telephonists will take the call and email you the message.

Fiverr - Fiverr is a website for global freelancers to pitch their services. I have used people on Fiverr for my business logos and things like t-shirt design. It can be quite inexpensive to get different aspects of design work completed. If you find a good freelancer, stick with them! They will get to know your business and be able to work really well with you.

Upwork is like Fiverr and you can go on and request freelancers to complete all types of work. I hired a copywriter in the USA a few years ago via the website. The way that it is set up is a little strange. You pay a deposit, set a brief and then other people pitch for the work. Even though this felt strange and I did feel sorry for whoever spent time pitching but not getting the job, it was good to see the variety of the responses. I scrolled through to figure out who I would connect with. This particular lady was really good so I wouldn't discount using the service again.

Connection Toolbag

I am not trying to teach anyone to suck eggs with these recommendations but for some people starting out in their own business for the very first time, the world of online calls and virtual meetings can seem daunting. Getting to grips with this technology can save valuable commuting time and get more done in less time with focused meetings with your business contacts. Since the pandemic of 2020, this has become the norm with virtual meetings replacing many face to face interactions.

Zoom - For around £15 per month, you can host your own virtual meeting rooms securely with no time limits and for up to 100 guests on each call. You can also host webinars through Zoom, but you will need to upgrade to the next level of payment.

Skype - This has been around for years. Conduct video calls and make telephone calls all over the world via Skype or top up your Skype credit to make international calls too.

Google meets - Like Zoom with variations for classrooms too. If like me, you are used to hosting in-person workshops, there are capabilities to host these online too if you ship out the materials to your course participants in advance.

Personal Tools

Shifting Your Energy

Feeling stuck and stagnant, whether that be on a particular task that has been niggling at you, or being stuck on an important business decision can seem frustrating. If procrastination is threatening to ruin your productivity and you need to get unstuck quickly, then a simple shift in energy is always my mode of choice.

If there is no time to exercise with a run, a long walk or perhaps a swim (for me swimming in the sea is a sure-fire way to shift my energy!) Then simply changing your body's energy as you work can suffice. Get up and move from your chair, walk, flail your arms around. What is your most favourite song in the whole world? Put it on and put it on loud. Dance, move, sing along. I use music a lot to energise me and shift that energy that keeps me stuck.

Spiritual Toolbag

I love the spiritual side of my personal life and love to blend this into my business too. Having a mindset that believes there is something out there greater than us all has been valuable in passing over my troubles and worries. I love to think that I can manifest anything I want in my life and business with true belief. I like to keep up my spiritual practice for my emotional and mental health. Here are some of the best spiritual tools that I use. Disclaimer: I know the 'woo' is not for everyone, so take this with a pinch of salt and take from it what you need.

Gaia App - Gaia is a subscription streaming service playing TV shows, documentaries and interviews from the leaders in science, health and well-being. Rather than binge-watching a series on Netflix, I really love to learn something new via the Gaia app. Maybe something to do with the brain or gut health or physics. There are also more holistic and spiritual practices showcased on the channel.

Moon App - We work in cycles in our lives. We have a daily cycle called our circadian rhythm, we have the cycle of our hormones, and we have cycles of the seasons. We also have the lunar cycle too. I have been tracking my energy and moods along with the lunar cycle via the Moon App. Considering we are 60% water and the moon has the capability to affect tides, it is not surprising that the moon can affect our energy too. The lunar cycle can sometimes explain why it is easy to do something one day and not the next. I like this because you know why you're being freaky! The app can tell you where the moon is in the lunar cycle and which star sign the new moon is in. I am not obsessive about it but like to check it. I am paying more attention to tracking both my energy and the lunar cycle using the app.

Crystals - Some people really love crystals in their home and office. Crystals are said to positively impact your body's energy field or chakras. My go-to crystals are Citrine known as the merchants stone for manifesting money and attracting new opportunities and creativity. Amethyst for intuition and higher wisdom, snowflake obsidian for protection and fluorite for learning and spirituality.

Meditation - I have been meditating for a few years now and get a sense of mental peace and clarity from taking the time to meditate. I first learned to meditate in a dedicated meditation class led by my friend Adele. It scared me at first as I went into the meditation very deeply. Now I love it and I am not frightened. It is relaxing and helps me think more clearly. I use the meditation app Insight Timer, my Gaia app or You Tube.

Singing Bowl - Singing bowls are used in meditation or yoga practice. Set to a certain frequency, they vibrate and produce rich tones. I have a large crystal singing bowl which you can run the soft mallet around the bowl to create the most powerful sound just like the bowl is singing. I use this to start and finish a meditation or Yoga session.

Oracle Cards - You can get oracle cards in many designs with different styles of messages and printed words, pictures and explanations. Like a deck of cards that you shuffle and pick at random, these sit on my desk and I draw one when I feel I need a message or a focus. The deck of cards come with inspiring messages accompanied by a book of explanations. I don't take a card every day but when I do it's incredibly accurate.

Dowsing Pendulum - A dowsing pendulum is typically a rock or crystal that hangs on the end of a string or chain. The pendulum is used as a way of gaining spiritual and material insight. I have a beautiful amethyst one that hangs on the end of a chain. Divining is the ancient practice of holding twigs or metal rods that are supposed to move in response to hidden objects. The practice of divining was often used to find sources of water or underground objects. The dowsing pendulum works with your subconscious and is a tool to be taken lightly as a form of divining. I ask my pendulum "Show me the sign for yes, show me the sign for no, show me the sign for maybe" and take a note of the direction and patterns that the pendulum takes. I use one to gain insight on a matter but remain open-minded. You have to be in a stable state, reasonable and open to hearing stuff that you might not want to hear. I ask my pendulum things like "Should I make these travel arrangements?" "Is it good for me to start this course?". I don't ask about others, only myself.

50 Top Tips for Entrepreneurs

A quick rapid-fire list for business owners that I swear by:

1. Eat the frog first - do the worst job first
2. Turn your notifications off
3. Don't multitask
4. Plan your day the day before
5. You can do anything but not everything
6. Do the most important jobs first
7. Just start and don't think about being perfect
8. Always carry a notebook and pen

9. Put a pen and paper by your bed for your creativity download

10. Get up early and work while everyone else is sleeping

11. Find a coach

12. No screens an hour before bed

13. When you are listening to Audible bump the speed up to x2

14. Outsource what you can't do

15. Meditate

16. Don't watch TV

17. Go on a news fast

18. Avoid negative people

19. Exercise every day

20. Be nice to everyone - even your haters

21. Read every day, motivational, developmental books only

22. Learn a new language

23. Writing something down is the first stage in manifesting

24. Don't complain about something you can't do anything about

25. When you check your emails action straight away, delete, do or delay

26. Put time aside to unsubscribe to emails

27. Don't add things to your 'to-do' list you have already done

28. Prioritise tasks

29. Use my 5-9 method to work on your side hustle

30. Always go to bed on the same day you get up

31. Write it down the second it's in your brain

32. Use apps to list tasks

33. Be aware when you are most productive in the day

34. Things are hardest just before they get better

35. Be true to your brand

36. Don't be pulled off-brand by people

37. Every journey begins with one step

38. Be disciplined so when you're not motivated you can still achieve

39. Always underpromise and over-deliver

40. Avoid hitting snooze

41. Take action

42. Ask for help

43. Don't give up

44. Set a deadline the day before it's needed

45. Ask for feedback

46. Listen to your customers

47. Make mistakes, but don't make the same one twice.

48. Communicate

49. Answer all emails

50. Get out of your comfort zone

Conclusion

Having been in business for the last decade, I have loved my journey both in my business endeavours and my personal growth and development.

As an avid reader, I know that I have consumed more non-fiction books in the last three years than I have in my whole life. I have thoroughly enjoyed reading about the stories and journeys of others. Some books you might only take away one small thing that impacts you. Other books might be a page-turning value-a-minute rollercoaster of lightbulb moments and knowledge bombs that change your life and your perspective. I love it when you're immersed in a book, and you're so engrossed, but something jumps out at you. It is so powerful that it makes you close the book, savour the information and nourish your brain with it.

My reading journey has inspired so much joy in my life. My continued curiosity has continued to thirst for new ideas and concepts and find that non-fiction helps to quench that thirst. I wanted to try and offer the most valuable things I have learned to others so that you too may be inspired into action. Whether that be a personal or business challenge, I want you to know that you are so much more capable than what you give credit for and you can achieve all of your goals in your life.

I wish you every success on your business and personal journey from this point. I would love for you to get in touch and tell me what you thought of my book. I read and reply to every email: jo@jomacfarlane.com.

Acknowledgements

Book dedication

This book is dedicated to the game-changer in you, the person who is going to put this book down and take action, you know there are things you need to go and do. You want something different, to dispel the haters and step outside your comfort zone. You might be the juiciest peach in the world but there is always someone who doesn't like peaches. If you gain one slice of a peach from this book my job is done.

Book acknowledgement

Thanks to my friend and collaborator the incredibly talented and dynamic Gemma Ray who without her this wouldn't have been possible. I asked the universe for someone to help me bring my dream of writing a self-help book to fruition and within the hour I was chatting to her on the phone. It looks like my dream just came true. I'm forever grateful.

To Stuart, thank you for putting up with the endless 5 am alarms, me making dinner far too late and my personal challenges that you know are so important to me and who I am. Thank you for never standing in the way of my dreams and being my partner on this great adventure that is life.

To Archie who bends my mind on a daily basis and inspires me to be a better person.

To my mum and dad, for bringing me into this world and making me the strong independent person I am.

To Heather and Johnny, I am forever grateful for everything you have done for me.

To Adele, you lit a path when I couldn't see. You led me into another world, I am forever grateful.

Lynne my running buddy for your constant positivity and endless chat that went on for 1000 miles and more.

To all my flying friends in BA for saving my ass on many occasions from racing room service trolleys down corridors and sitting on meal trays at the front of the plane on the take-off roll (no passengers) to see who could go the fastest.

To my wonderful inspirational 'Ignite Tribe' you rock!

To all my beautiful candlemakers who have attended over the many years at Candletowers.
Not so many thanks to my hens who kept me out of flow with their never-ending escape tricks, without those I might have written this book years ago!

Printed in Great Britain
by Amazon

56902915R00136